The Book of Concealed Mystery

God creates light. Engraving by H Pisan after Gustave Doré (1832-83).

Ways of Mysticism

The Book of
Concealed
Mystery

CONTINUUM

About the illustrations

The illustrations in the Introduction are from the original edition.
The illustration which opens each chapter showing the religious
symbols of Judaism is from Jericho and is from an ancient synagogue
mosaic floor dating from the sixth or seventh centuries BCE.

The Publisher acknowledges the following for use of their
illustrations: e.t. archive: 91; Mary Evans Picture Library:
2,6,40,56,68,74,86; Fortean Picture Library: 14,78,82.

Continuum Publishing Inc.
Wellington House, 125 Strand, London WC2R 0BB
320 Lexington Avenue, New York, NY 10017-6550, USA

This edition first published in 1926 by Routledge and Kegan Paul as
part of *The Kabbalah Unveiled*
Translated by S L MacGregor Mathers

© Copyright. This re-designed and illustrated edition
Delian Bower Publishing 2000

First published 2000 in the Ways of Mysticism Series

ISBN 0826449972

A·Delian·Bower·Book
Edited, designed and produced by
Delian Bower Publishing
Exeter England

Designed by Vic Giolitto
Picture research by Anne-Marie Ehrlich

Printed in China

Contents

The Tree of Life of the Kabbalah. A sixteenth-century engraving.

Introduction

*T*he Book of Concealed Mystery is one of the eighteen parts of *The Zohar (The Book of Splendour)* written towards the end of the thirteenth century and thought to be the work of Moses of Leon. Essentially a commentary on the Torah (Law), it is considered to be the primary source of our knowledge about Jewish kabbalism.

Kabbalists believe that God is Absolute, Divine, Limitless, and Infinite. They also perceive Him as the Ain Soph - the First Cause and cause of causes. The Ain Soph underlies everything and links everything together. But at the same time is beyond understanding and definition. This would seem to be a paradox. How is the Universe and humankind to be explained if it is beyond our understanding?

In seeing the Ain Soph as the First Cause, the kabbalists also believe that the universe and all that is in it is an expression of the Divine Will or Wisdom. The finite has no existence except in the light of the Infinite. The Universe emanates from God in successive layers called the Sephiroth in whom He is present though He transcends humankind.

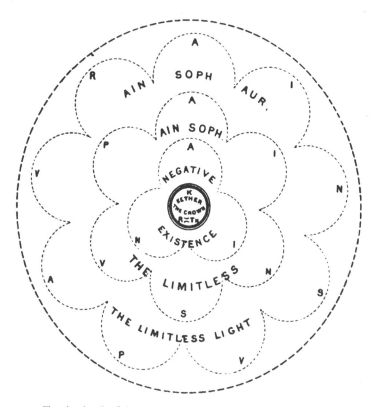

The cloud-veils of the Ain Soph formulating the hidden Sephiroth.
Concentrating in Kether, the First Sephira.

The Book of Concealed Mystery is so called because it asserts that the light of God, the Infinite must be concealed in order to be revealed. Even though kabbalists believe that God is beyond understanding, contemplation of Him and prayer to Him, who is present in all things, can transform our minds and thoughts and bring us closer to Him

The present work was translated by S.L. MacGregor Mathers in 1887 from the Latin version of Knorr von Rosenthoth and collated with the original Chaldee and Hebrew text. Its original title *The Kabbalah Unveiled* also included two other parts of *The Zohar*: *The Greater Holy Assembly* and *The Lesser Holy Assembly.* However, *The Book of Concealed Mystery,* which is concerned with the beginnings of things and the creation of the world, is considered to be the root and foundation of *The Zohar.*

In the original Introduction MacGregor Mathers states:

'*The Book of Concealed Mystery* is the book of the equilibrium of balance.' What is here meant by the terms "equilibrium of balance"? Equilibrium is that harmony which results from the analogy of contraries, it is the dead centre where, the opposition of opposing forces being equal in strength, rest succeeds motion. It is the central point. It is the "point within the circle" of ancient symbolism. It is the living synthesis of counterbalanced power. Thus form may be described as the equilibrium of light and shade; take away either factor, and form is viewless. The term balance is applied to the two opposite natures in each triad of the Sephiroth, their equilibrium forming the third Sephira in each ternary. I shall recur again to this subject in explaining the Sephiroth. This doctrine of equilibrium and balance is a fundamental kabalistical idea.'

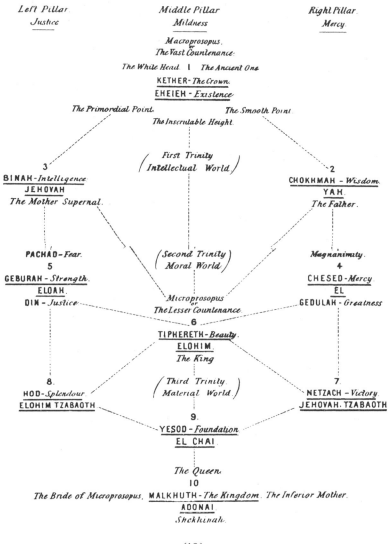

THE SEPHIROTH.
AIN SOPH THE LIMITLESS ONE.

Left Pillar.
Justice

Middle Pillar
Mildness

Right Pillar.
Mercy.

Macroprosopus.
or
The Vast Countenance.

The White Head. | The Ancient One.

KETHER- *The Crown.*

EHEIEH - *Existence*

The Primordial Point.   The Smooth Point.

The Inscrutable Height.

*First Trinity
Intellectual World*

3   2
BINAH-*Intelligence.*   CHOKHMAH - *Wisdom.*
JEHOVAH   YAH.
The Mother Supernal.   The Father.

PACHAD- *Fear.*   Magnanimity.
5   4
GEBURAH - *Strength.*   CHESED - *Mercy.*
ELOAH.   EL.
DIN - *Justice*   *Second Trinity   GEDULAH - Greatness*
                          Moral World

Microprosopus
or
The Lesser Countenance.

6

TIPHERETH - *Beauty.*
ELOHIM.
The King

8.   *Third Trinity.   7.*
HOD- *Splendour.*   *Material World*   NETZACH – *Victory.*
ELOHIM TZABAOTH.   JEHOVAH. TZABAOTH.

9.

YESOD - *Foundation.*
EL CHAI.

The Queen
10
The Bride of Microprosopus,   MALKHUTH- *The Kingdom.* The Inferior Mother.
ADONAI.
Shekhinah.

He goes on to explain the hidden ideas of the Sephiroth

'... There are three kabalistical veils of the negative existence, and in themselves they formulate the *hidden* ideas of the Sephiroth not yet called into being, and they are concentrated in Kether, which in this sense is the Malkuth of tho hidden ideas of the Sephiroth. I will explain this. The first veil of the negative existence is the AIN, *Ain* negativity. This word consists of three letters, which thus shadow forth the first three Sephiroth or numbers. The second veil is the AIN SVP, *Ain Soph* = the Limitless. This title consists of six letters, and shadows forth the idea of the first six Sephiroth or numbers. The third veil is the AIN SVP AVR, *Ain Soph Aur* = the Limitless Light. This again consists of nine letters, and symbolises the first nine Sephiroth, but of course in their hidden idea only. But when we reach the number nine we cannot progress further without returning to the unity, of the number one, for the number ten is but a repetition of unity freshly derived from the negative, as is evident from a glance at its ordinary representation in Arabic numerals, where the circle O represents the Negative, and the 1 the Unity. Thus, then, tho limitless ocean of negative light *does not proceed from a centre, for it is centreless, but it concentrates a centre* which is the number one of the manifested Sephiroth, - Kether, the Crown, the First Sephira; which therefore may be said to be the Malkuth or number ten of the hidden Sephiroth. (See page 8).

'... I must now explain the real meaning of the terms Sephira and Sephiroth. The first is singular, the second is plural. Tho best rendering of the word is "numerical emanation." There are ten Sephiroth, which are the most abstract forms of the ten numbers of the decimal scale i.e., the numbers i.e. 1, 2, 3, 4, 5, 6, 7, 8, 9, 1O. Therefore, as

PLATE I.—TABLE OF HEBREW AND CHALDEE LETTERS.

Number	Sound or Power	Hebrew and Chaldee Letters	Numerical Value	Roman character by which expressed in this work	Name	Signification of Name.
1.	a (soft breathing).		1. (Thousands are	A.	Aleph.	Ox.
2.	b, bh (v).		2. denoted by a	B.	Beth.	House.
3.	g (hard), gh.		3. larger letter;	G.	Gimel.	Camel.
4.	d, dh (flat th).		4. thus an Aleph	D.	Daleth.	Door.
5.	h (rough breathing).		5. larger than the	H.	He.	Window.
6.	v, u, o.		6. rest of the let-	V.	Vau.	Peg, nail.
7.	s, dz.		7. ters among	Z.	Zayin.	Weapon, sword.
8.	ch (guttural).		8. which it is,	Ch.	Cheth.	Enclosure, fence.
9.	t (strong).		9. signifies not 1,	T.	Teth.	Serpent.
10.	i, y (as in yes).		10. but 1000.)	I.	Yod.	Hand.
11.	k, kh.	Final =	20. Final = 500	K.	Caph.	Palm of the hand.
12.	l.		30.	L.	Lamed.	Ox-goad.
13.	m.	Final =	40. Final = 600	M.	Mem.	Water.
14.	n.	Final =	50. Final = 700	N.	Nun.	Fish.
15.	s.		60.	S.	Samekh.	Prop, support.
16.	O, aa, ng (gutt.).		70.	O.	Ayin.	Eye.
17.	p, ph.	Final =	80. Final = 800	P.	Pe.	Mouth.
18.	ts, tz, j.	Final =	90. Final = 900	Tz.	Tzaddi.	Fishing-hook.
19.	q, qh (guttur.).		100. (The finals are not	Q.	Qoph.	Back of the head.
20.	r.		200. always considered	R.	Resh.	Head.
21.	sh, s.		300. as bearing an in-	Sh.	Shin.	Tooth.
22.	th, t.		400. creased numeri- cal value.)	Th.	Tau.	Sign of the cross.

in the higher mathematics we reason of numbers in their abstract sense, so in the Kabbalah we reason of the Deity by the abstract forms of the numbers;in other words, by the SPIRVTh, Sephiroth. It was from this ancient Oriental theory that Pythagoras derived his numerical symbolic ideas.' (See Table on page 12).

The original notes integrated within the text in smaller type are included as they are an invaluable commentary and will help clarify our understanding. As there are a number of Hebrew or Chaldee words in the text, the Table on page 12 indicates the Hebrew and Chaldee alphabet (which is common to both languages) and the equivalent in Roman characters. The Table also indicates their names, powers and numerical values. There are no separate numerical characters in Hebrew and Chaldee; therefore as is also the case in Greek, each letter has its own peculiar numerical value.

The reader should also refer to the Glossary on page 92 for further clarification of words and terms used.

For this edition a selection of illustrations have been included to compliment the text.

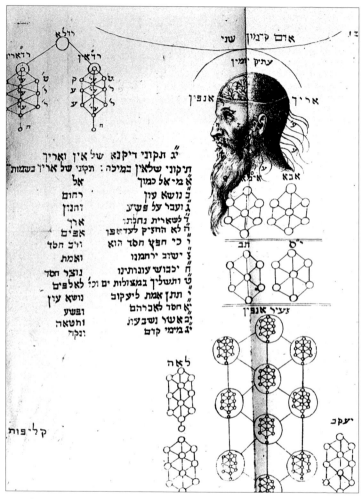

'The Ancient of Days' or 'The Great Head of Zohar'. An illustration from a seventeenth-century Kabbalist treatise.

CHAPTER 1

*T*he Book of Concealed Mystery (*Siphra Dtzenioutha*)
is the book of the equilibrium of balance.

The word 'Dtzenioutha' is difficult to translate, but I think its
meaning is best expressed by the words *Concealed Mystery*. The
Book of Concealed Mystery opens with these words: 'The Book of
Concealed Mystery is the book of the equilibrium of balance.'
What is here meant by the terms 'equilibrium of balance'?
Equilibrium is that harmony which results from the analogy of
contraries, it is the dead centre where, the opposition of opposing
forces being equal in strength, rest succeeds motion. It is the central point. It is the 'point within the circle' of ancient symbolism. It
is the living synthesis of counterbalanced power. Thus form may be
described as the equilibrium of light and shade; take away either
factor, and form is viewless. The term balance is applied to the two
opposite natures in each triad of the Sephiroth, their equilibrium
forming the third Sephira in each ternary. I shall recur again to this
subject in explaining the Sephiroth. This doctrine of equilibrium
and balance is a fundamental qabalistical idea.

For before there was equilibrium, countenance beheld not
countenance.

And the kings of ancient time were dead, and their
crowns were found no more; and the earth was desolate.

The 'kings of ancient time' mean the same thing as the 'Edomite
Kings;' that is, they symbolize worlds of 'unbalanced force,' which,

according to the Zohar, preceded the formation of this universe.

Until that head (which is incomprehensible) desired by all desires (proceeding from AIN SVP, *Ain Soph*, the infinite and limitless one), appeared and communicated the vestments of honour.

> This Head, which is here described as proceeding from the infinite and limitless One, the *Ain Soph*, is the first Sephira, the Crown *Kether*, otherwise called *Arikh Anpin*, or Macroprosopus, the Vast Countenance. From this first Sephira the other nine emanations are produced.

This equilibrium hangs in that region which is negatively existent in the Ancient One.

> By the expression 'This equilibrium hangs in that region which is negatively existent in the Ancient One,' is meant that the other nine Sephiroth (which are equilibrated by their formation in trinities) are as yet not developed in the first Sephira, but exist within it as the tree exists in the seed from which it springs. By 'the Ancient One' is intended the first Sephira, the Crown Kether, one of whose appellations is *Autheqa*, the Ancient One.

Thus did those powers proceed which were not yet in perceptible existence.

> These powers are the other nine Sephiroth, which are, as it were, powers of the first Sephira; as soon as they are equated they become positively existent through correlation of force. The next two sections explain the manner of their equilibration while yet negative entities, or rather ideas.

In His form (in the form of the Ancient One) exists the equilibrium: it is incomprehensible, it is unseen.

> But the first idea of equilibrium is the Ancient One (the first Sephira, or Crown Kether), because it is the first potential limita-

tion of the boundless light which proceeds from the Limitless One. That is, the central point of Kether is the equilibrium, because the balance does not yet exist, the two opposite poles which form the balance not being yet developed. We must not confuse these two terms, equilibrium and balance. The balance consists of two scales (opposing forces), the equilibrium is the central point of the beam.

Therein have they ascended, and therein do they ascend—they who are not, who are, and who shall be.

Therein (in the equilibrium of Kether) have they ascended (developed when they became positively existent), and therein (in the equilibrium) do they ascend (have their first existence), they (the Sephiroth) who are not (exist negatively), who are (then become positive), and who shall be (exist permanently, because they are counterbalanced powers). This triple expression 'are not, are, and shall be,' also refers to the triple trinity of the Sephiroth.

The head which is incomprehensible is secret in secret.

This head is Macroprosopus, the Vast Countenance, and is the same as the Ancient One, or Crown Kether. It is secret, for therein are hidden the other potentialities.

But it has been formed and prepared in the likeness of a cranium, and is filled with the crystalline dew.

The crystalline dew is the creative lux or *Aur*, , proceeding from the Limitless One. The Mantuan Codex calls the skull or cranium the first, and the crystalline dew the second conformation of Macroprosopus.

His skin is of ether, clear and congealed.

(His hair is as) most fine wool, floating through the balanced equilibrium.

The ether is the clear and insupportable brilliance of his glory. The hair is white—i.e.; spotless as wool—to denote the utter absence of matter and of shell. The Mantuan Codex calls the ether the third conformation, and the hair the fourth, which latter it refers to the Sephira Netzach, victory.

(His forehead is) the benevolence of those benevolences which are manifested through the prayers of the inferior powers.

The supernal benignity which transmits their qualities, powers and offices, to the lower Sephiroth (the inferior powers). It must be remembered that each Sephira *receives from* that which immediately precedes it, and *transmits* to that which next follows it. Thus, each Sephira is said to be feminine or passive as regards its predecessor, and masculine or active in respect to its successor. The Mantuan Codex calls this the fifth conformation, and refers it to the idea of the ninth Sephira, Yesod, foundation.

His eye is ever open and does not sleep, for it continually keeps watch. And the appearance of the lower is according to the aspect of the higher light.

Were the eye to close (the directing thought Divine to be abstracted from the Sephiroth), the whole universe would give way, for its mainspring would be withdrawn. Because the appearance (development) of the lower (nine Sephiroth) is according to (dependent on) the aspect (ruling thought) of the higher light (Kether, the first Sephira). The Mantuan Codex terms this the sixth conformation of Macroprosopus, and refers it, as in the case of the fourth conformation, to the primal idea of the Sephira Netzach, victory.

Therein are His two nostrils like mighty galleries, from where His spirit rushes forth over all. (The Mantuan Codex adds that this is the seventh conformation, which refers to, *Malkuth*, or 'the kingdom,' the tenth emanation or Sephira of the Deity.)

The creative spirit, or the 'breath of life.'

(When, therefore, the Divine law begins) BRAShITh BRA ALHIM ATh HShMIM VATh HARTz, *Berashith Bera Elohim Ath Hashamaim Vaath Haaretz:* 'In the beginning the Elohim created the substance of the heavens and the substance of the earth.' (The sense is: Six members were created, which are the six numerations of Microprosopus—viz., benignity as His right arm; severity as His left arm; beauty as His body; victory as His right leg; glory as His left leg; and the foundation as reproductive.) For instead of BRAShITh, *Berashith,* 'in the beginning,' it may be read, BRA ShITh, *Bera Shith,* 'He created the six.' Upon these depend all things which are below (principally the Queen, who is the lowest path, or the bride of Microprosopus, and all the three inferior worlds.)

> The view which the Siphra Dtzenioutha here follows out is that the beginning of Genesis describes *not only the creation of the world. but the development of God,* for it considers the universe as the outward and material expression of the power of the thought Divine. Microprosopus is as it were the reflection of Macroprosopus, for as Macroprosopus has six principal titles, so is Microprosopus composed of six of the Sephiroth. ShITh, *Shith,* is the Chaldee form of the Hebrew ShSh, *Shash,* six. The queen is Malkuth, the tenth Sephira. The three inferior worlds are Briah, Yetzirah, and Asiah.

And the dignity of dignity hangs from the seven conformations of the cranium. (This is the beard of the venerable and Ancient One, which is divided into thirteen portions).

> The Ancient One is the first Sephira, Macroprosopus. The beard, in continuation of the symbolic representation of the head, is divided into thirteen portions, which answer by Gematria to the idea of unity. For AChD *Achad,* unity, yields the number 13 by numerical value.

And the second earth came not into the computation. (That is, the kingdom of the restored world, which elsewhere is called the Bride of Microprosopus, came not into the computation when the six members were said to be created. Or otherwise, when in Genesis 4, 2 it is said in another way, 'And the earth,' that earth is not to be understood of which mention has been first made; since by the first is to be understood the kingdom of the restored world, and by the second the kingdom of the destroyed world), and this is elsewhere said.

> The kingdom of the destroyed world is that of unbalanced force. This refers to a period prior to the development of the Sephiroth, and must therefore be referable to the Edomite kings.

And it has proceeded out of that which has undergone the curse, as it is written in Genesis 5, 29, 'From the earth which the Lord has cursed.' (The meaning is: That the kingdom of the restored world was formed from the kingdom of the destroyed world, wherein seven kings had died and their possessions had been broken up. Or, the explanation of the world, of which mention is made elsewhere, proceeds from the kingdom of the destroyed world.)

> These seven kings are the Edomite kings mentioned on page 15.

It was formless and void, and darkness upon the face of the deep, and the Spirit of the Elohim vibrating upon the face of the waters. Thirteen (these words, from 'it was formless' down to 'of the waters,' are thirteen in the Hebrew text of Genesis) depend from the thirteen (forms) of the dignity of dignity (that is, the beard of the Macroprosopus, or first formed head).

> I have before remarked that the number thirteen expresses unity.

The author of *The Book of Concealed Mystery* here argues that the very number and order of the words in the Hebrew text refer to certain forms of the Deity. The terms 'face of the deep' and 'face of the waters' bear a striking analogy to Macroprosopus and Microprosopus, the Vast and the Lesser Countenances. In this sense the 'face of (from) the deep (abyss)' is the countenance formed from Ain Soph, the Limitless One; namely, the first Sephira, the Crown Kether.

Six thousand years depend from the six first. This is what the wise have said, that the world shall last six thousand years, and it is understood from the six numbers of Microprosopus. But also the six following words give occasion to this idea: VIAMR ALHIM IHI AVR VIHI AVR, Veyomar Elohim Yehi Aur Vayehi Aur: 'And the Elohim said, Let there be light, and there was light.'

By an exegetical rule of numbers, not so often employed as the others, simple numbers or units signify divine things; numbers of ten, celestial things; numbers of a hundred, terrestrial things; and thousands signify the future, what shall be in an after-age. Hence are the 'six thousand years' deduced from the six first words, which also are said to refer to the six Sephiroth of whom Microprosopus is formed; the idea of six being extended into as many thousands, to symbolise that number on the plane of a future age.

The seventh (the millennium, and the seventh space, namely, the Kingdom), above that One which alone is powerful—(i.e., when the six degrees of the members denote mercies and judgments, the seventh degree tends alone to judgment and rigour). And the whole is desolate (that is, the Kingdom, MLKVTH, *Malkuth*, in the higher powers, is the antitype of the sanctuary, and like as this is destroyed, so also the Schechinah, or Kingdom, is itself exiled) for twelve hours (for the Hebrews include all this time of their exile in the space of one day). Like as it is written: 'It was formless and void, &c.' (for from the word 'it was formless,' down to 'upon the faces of,' are twelve words in the Hebrew text of Genesis.)

> By the same rule, the millennium is deduced from the seventh word. The seventh space here means Malkuth, the kingdom, or the queen, which together with the six of Microprosopus, makes up the seven lower Sephiroth.

The thirteenth (that is, 'of the waters,' HMIM, *Hamim*, which is the thirteenth word) raises up these (that is, as well the sanctuary which is above as that which is below) through mercy (since the water symbolizes that measure of mercy through which judgment and punishments are mitigated), and they are renewed as before (for the six words follow afresh, as in the beginning the six members are enumerated). For all those six continue and stand fast (they are the members of the Microprosopus, and are not as his bride, and from them is the restitution), since it is written, BRA, *Bera*, 'created' (which has a sense of permanence), and then it is written HIThH, *Hayitha*, 'it was' (which also is a phrase of permanence and not of interpolation), for it is very truth (plainly, therefore, the kingdom perished not, although it might be formless and void, but it retains hitherto the essence).

> Mercy and judgment are opposites, and from the side of judgment comes the execution of judgment, which is destruction.

And at the end of the Formless and the Void and the Darkness (that is, at the end of the exile this saying shall have place: Isa. 2, 11). And the Tetragrammaton alone shall be exalted in that day (that is, in the time of Messiah).

The Tetragrammaton comprehends the whole ten Sephiroth, and
consequently expresses their three trinities of balanced force also;
consequently, when the Tetragrammaton appears, the formless and
the void and the darkness disappear, and form, fulness, and light
replace them.

But there are excavations of excavations. (The excavation
is the receptacle, like that which is hollowed out, or carved
out, like a cave, or any other receptacle. Therefore all
receptacles are inferior with respect to the superiors,
among which the 'shells' hold the last place, which here
are described, which are) under the form of a vast serpent
extending this way and that. (Concerning this serpent the
author of the *Royal Valley* speaks thus in his *Treatise of
the Shells*. The fragments of the receptacles, which have
fallen into the world of Creation, of Formation, and of
Action, therein exist from the Outer; and judgments are
more consonant to these, which are called profane, and
have their habitation in the middle space between the
Holy and the Unclean. And from the head is formed that
great dragon which is in the sea, and is the sea-serpent,
which is, however, not so harmful as the earthly one. And
this dragon has been castrated since his crest (or *mem-
brum genitale*), together with his mate, have been
repressed, and thence, have been formed four hundred
desirable worlds. And this dragon has in his head a nostril
(after the manner of whales) in order that he may receive
influence, and in himself he contains all other dragons,
concerning which it is said: 'You have broken the heads of
the dragons upon the waters' (Ps. 74, 13). And here the
idea or universal form of all the shells is understood,
which encompasses the seven inferior emanations of the
queen after the manner of a serpent, as well from the right
as from the left and from every side.)

The excavation or receptacle of a Sephira is that quality whereby it receives the supernal influence from that which immediately precedes it; hence each Sephira has a double quality of receiving and of transmitting, which passes through the four worlds in each of which the Sephiroth exist, though in gradually decreasing light. (See Diagrams on pp. 8,10) The 'shells,' *Qlipoth*, are the demons, in whom again is a form of the Sephiroth, distorted and averse. This great dragon which is here described is evidently identical with the leviathan of Job. He is the executor of judgment, the centripetal force, the old serpent ever seeking to penetrate into Paradise; finally, in a more *exoteric* sense he is Satan and the devil, the accusing one. In the *Sepher Yetzirah*, a most important qabalistical book, he is called *Theli*, ThLI, the dragon. Now, by Gematria, ThLI = 400 + 30 + 10 = 440; and if we 'repress his crest'—i.e., take away the first letter, which is Th, *Tau*,—400, there will remain LI = 40 = M, *Mem*, the water. The '400 desirable worlds' are the numerical value of Th, and signify the power of the Tetragrammaton on the material plane (See pages 8,10). There is much alchemical symbolism contained in the 'Siphra Dtzenioutha.' The 'Seven Inferior Emanations' of the queen, are the seven lower Sephiroth—viz., Chesed, Geburah, Tiphereth, Netzach, Hod, Yesod, and Malkuth; or Microprosopus and his bride, the king and queen. 'Shells,' *Qlipoth*, are the evil spirits.

His tail is in his head (that is, he holds his tail in his mouth, in order that he may form a circle, since he is said to encompass holiness). He transfers his head to behind the shoulders (that is, he raises his head at the back of the bride of Microprosopus, where is the place of most severe judgments), and he is despised (since in him is the extremity of judgments and severities, from where wrath is the attribute of his forms). He watches (that is, he accurately searches out and seeks in what place he may gain an entry into holiness. And he is concealed (as if laying traps; since he insinuates himself into the inferiors, by whose sins he has access to the holy grades, where the carrying out of judgments is committed to him). He is manifested in one of the thousand shorter days. (Numbers are called days, and numbers of the inferior world short days; among which tens are attributed to the factive, on account of their decimal numeration; hundreds to the formative, since they are numbers of the light of their author, and draw their existence from the tens; but thousands to the creative, for the same reason. But that dragon has about this his most powerful location, from where, if a defect occurs only in one numeration of that system through the fault of the inferiors, he is immediately manifest, and thus commences his accusations before the throne of glory.)

Here is the origin of the well-known symbol of a serpent holding his tail in his mouth, like a circle—the serpent of Saturn. The reason that he raises his head behind the shoulders of the bride (Malkuth) is because he is, so to speak, not only the executor of judgment. but also the destroyer; destruction as opposed to creation, death as opposed to life. For the whole Sephiroth are represented as being the balance of mercy and justice, and the tenth Sephira is especially of the nature of justice, as also is Geburah, the fifth. He is concealed, because he is not called into action till justice requires him. The term 'decimal numeration' of course refers to the ten Sephiroth. The presence of the serpent when revealed, is an accusation, because it shows that the balance is destroyed; just as in a watch, if one of the wheels be injured, irregularity is at once manifested. Now, life, when it consists of birth into another form, necessarily implies death in the previous form. The throne of glory is the Briatic world.

There are swellings in his scales (that is, like as in a crocodile; because great in him is the heaping together of judgments). His crest keeps its own place (that is, there is in him no further power of hastening to things beyond in the Outer).

There is in the destroyer no 'hastening to the outer,' because he is centripetal and not centrifugal.

But his head is broken by the waters of the great sea. (The great sea is wisdom, the fountain of mercy and loving kindness; which, if it sends down its influence, judgments are pacified, and the hurtful power of the shells is restricted); like as it is written, Ps. 74, 13: 'You have broken the heads of the dragons by the waters.'

'The waters of the great sea,' are the influence of the supernal mother, Binah, of whom Malkuth is the reflection. But Binah receives the influence of Chokmah.

They were two (male and female, whence the text of the Psalm speaks of the dragons in the plural number; but when the plural number is given in its least form, two only are understood). They are reduced into one (for the female leviathan has been slain, lest they should seek to multiply judgments). The word ThNINM, *Thenanim* (in the before-mentioned passage of the Psalm), is written in a defective form (purposely to denote that restriction).

I may refer the reader to the Talmud for further information regarding Jewish ideas of the Leviathan.

(But it is said) heads (in the plural number, for the purpose of denoting a vast multitude, as well of species as of individuals in that genus); like as it is written, Ezek. 1, 22: 'And a likeness as a firmament above the heads of the living creature.' (Where also the word living creature, ChIH, *Chiah*, is put in the singular as a genus of angels; and heads in the plural for the purpose of denoting species and innumerable individuals.)

'You have broken the heads of the dragons (*Thenanim*) by the waters.' It must be remembered that this dragon is said by the author of the 'Royal Valley' to be the king of all the 'shells' or demons. Now, the demons are divided into ten classes, corresponding to the ten Sephiroth, but in an averse form, and are called in the book, 'Beth Elohim,' the 'impure Sephiroth.' The heads of the leviathan (cf. the Lernan Hydra which Hercules slew) are probably these. Compare the description of the beast in the Book of Revelation.

'And the Elohim said, let there be light, and there was light.' (The sense may be sought from that Psalm 33, 9) where it is written, 'Since He Himself spoke, and it was done.' (First, therefore, is commemorated) the Path HVA, *Hoa*, (that is, the mother of understanding, who is called ALHIM *Elohim*, near the beginning of the verse. 'And the Elohim said.' She also is called HVA, *Hoa*, in the words of Psalm 33, 9, on account of her truly secret nature) is alone (as well with Moses as with David). The word VIHI, *Vayehi*, 'and it was done,' is also alone. (As if the six members were considered separately, seeing that V, *Vau*, occupied the first place in the word VIHI, *Vayehi*.

This statement, that the supernal mother symbolized by the word Hoa, He, seems at first sight at variance with the statement in another place, that Hoa represents Macroprosopus. But the letter H in the Tetragrammaton symbolizes the supernal mother, and this is also the initial letter of Hoa. And again by Gematria (see Introduction) Hoa, HVA = 5 + 6 + 1 = 12, and the digits of 12 1 + 2 = 3. And 3 symbolizes Binah because she is the third Sephira. 'Seeing that V, Vau, occupies the first place in the word Vau because V stands for the number 6.

Then are the letters inverted, and become one. (If, namely, in the word VIHI, *Vayehi*, the letters I, *Yod*, and H, *He*, be placed in front so that it may read HIVI, *Yahevi*, it makes one Tetragrammaton, which exhausts the whole Divinity. But since these belong to the mother, from whom arise the judgments, hence this tetragrammaton is here written in retrograde order, which mode of writing is referred by qabalists to the judgments, on account of the nature of averse things; whence this ought to be written in this way: IHVI, *Yahevi,* IHV, *Yeho,* IH, *Yah,* I, *Yod.* But since in the path of understanding those judgments themselves do not exist, but only their roots, while in itself this path is only pure mercy; hence the retrograde order is inverted, in order that it may be posited entire in this manner as at first): I, *Yod,* IH, *Yah,* IHV, *Yeho,* IHVI, *Yahevi.* (But it is not written in the usual manner, IHVH, *Yod, He, Vau, He;* because the word is derived from VIHI, *Vayehi,* whose metathesis is here discussed. And nevertheless the letter) which is last (namely, I, *Yod,* which is put in the place of the last H, *He,* in the ordinary form of the Tetragrammaton, denotes), the Schechinah (or the queenly presence) which is below (that is, a path of the kingdom, namely, MLKVTh, *Malkuth,* the tenth and last Sephira); like as (in the other instance) the letter H, *He,* is found to be the Schechinah.

Any four-lettered name is of course a tetragrammaton, but this term is especially applied to the word of four letters called by biblical translators Jehovah. It must be remembered that the natural course of writing Hebrew and Chaldee is from *right to left,* and that when it is written from *left to right,* it is said to be written 'backwards,' 'in retrograde order,' or 'averse.' By the 'path of understanding' is meant Binah, the third Sephira. Schechinah is of course the Divine Presence manifested in the path of Malkuth.

But in one balance are they equiponderated. (The balance denotes the male and the female; and the meaning is, that the letters I, *Yod,* and H, *He* – of which the former is masculine and refers to the path of the foundation; and the latter is feminine, pertaining to the queen—are interchangeable; since whilst the equilibrium exists there is an intercommunication between them, and they are joined together as one. Add to this that the queen is also called ADNI, *Adonaï,* where I, *Yod,* brings up the rearguard of the army, as it were; because also it is accustomed to be called the Lesser Wisdom.) And the living creatures rush forth and return. (This is what is said in Ezek. 1, 14 concerning the living creatures, which it is accustomed to be said concerning those letters of the Tetragrammaton, which sometimes hold the last place and sometimes the first; as when I, *Yod*, rushes forth unto the last place, and when it returns unto the beginning again; and so also H, *He*. Likewise, then, also the living creatures are said to rush forth, when the Tetragrammaton is written with the final H, *He*, because then the whole system of emanatives is exhausted. But they are said to return when the Tetragrammaton is written with the final I, *Yod*, so that the sense may be collected in such a manner as to return from the last path of the queen into the penultimate of the foundation, which is designated by this letter I, *Yod*.

> The 'path of the foundation' is of course Yesod, the ninth Sephira, while the queen is Malkuth, the tenth, Yesod is therefore the connecting link between the Microprosopus and the bride. The letter I 'brings up the rearguard as it were' in the name ADNI, *Adonai*, because it is the last letter. Ezek, 1, 14: the Qabalists by the term ChIVTh HQDSh, *Chaioth Ha-Qadesch*, the Holy Living-Creatures, understand the letters of the Tetragrammaton. With regard to the 'letters of the Tetragrammaton, which sometimes hold the last place and sometimes the first,' the following are two examples—namely, as in the form IHVI, *Yod, He, Vau, Yod*, the letter I, *Yod*, is both at the beginning and end of the word; and in the form which is more usual IHVH, *Yod, He, Vau, He*, the letter H, *He*, is in the second and last place.

Like as it is written: 'And the Elohim saw the substance of the light, that it was good. (Here a reason is adduced from the proposed text itself, showing how the last letter of this form of the Tetragrammaton, namely, I, *Yod*, may be said to symbolize the bride, since God himself might behold in that light the path of conjunctive foundation, which the word 'goodness' points out; but when the foundation is in the act of conjunction—that is, under the idea of communicating goodness—there then is the bride. But also that the word 'goodness' denotes the foundation is proved from Isa, 3, 10, where it is said, 'Say to the righteous man' (that is, to the path of foundation, because the first man is said to be the foundation of the world, Prov. 10, 25), 'that it shall be well with him.' Therefore, then do they ascend within the equilibrium. (That is, these two letters, I, *Yod*, and H, *He*, mean one and the same thing. Or, again: But behold, how in balanced power ascend the letters of Tetragrammaton. That is, how those letters agree when in conjunction, which before were standing separated in the word VIHI, *Vayehi*.)

> The 'path of foundation' is of course the ninth Sephira, Yesod, which is the sixth member of Microprosopus (see p.10), and typifies reproductive power. Malkuth is the queen. We must remember that in the Tetragrammaton, IHVH, I, *Yod* is the father (who is not Macroprosopus, though he is implied therein, as the top point of the Hebrew letter Yod is said to symbolize him); H, *He*, the supernal mother; V, *Vau*, the son (Microprosopus); and H, *He*, final, the bride (the queen). And this is their proper order. Other variations of the Tetragrammaton, therefore, alter the position of the letters with regard to each other; their normal and correct position being IHVH.

(Whilst the spouse, Microprosopus) was at first alone (he was standing by, whilst the letter V, *Vau*, occupied the first place, then was he separated from his bride). But all things returned into the unity. (That is, not only were father and mother conjoined into one, because the two letters, I, *Yod*, and H, *He*, were combined; but also the Microprosopus returned to his bride, whilst V, *Vau*, was placed next to I, *Yod*, in the Tetragrammaton, IHVI, *Yahevi*. For) V, *Vau*, descended (when in the word VIHI, *Vayehi*, 'and it was done,' it occupied the first place; but in the proposed metathesis, it descended into the third place, in order that it might be IHVI, *Yahevi*). And they are bound together the one to the other (male and female, V, *Vau*, and I, *Yod*, the path of beauty and the queen), namely, I, *Yod*, and H, *He* (by which are shown wisdom and knowledge, father and mother), like unto two lovers who embrace each other. (By two lovers are understood either V, *Vau*, and I, *Yod*, only—that is, at the end; or I, *Yod*, and H, *He*, together—that is, at the beginning).

> The 'path of beauty,' or Tiphereth, the sixth Sephira, is sometimes represented by V, *Vau*, and therefore sometimes stands for Microprosopus by itself; it is really the *central* Sephira of the group of six Sephiroth which compose him. The numerical value of Vau is 6.

(Now the author of *The Book of Concealed Mystery* hastens to the latter explanation of these letters, 1, *Yod*; and V, *Vau*; and concerning V, *Vau*, he says): Six members are produced from the branch of the root of his body. (The body is Microprosopus; the root of the body is the mother, who is symbolized by the letter H, *He*; the branch of the root is the letter V, *Vau*, enclosed and hidden within the letter H, *He*; and from that very branch were produced the six members—that is, the entire letter V, *Vau*, now having obtained the head.)

> The mother here mentioned is of course the third Sephira, Binah. The six members of Microprosopus forming the entire letter Vau is an allusion to the numerical value of that letter being 6.

'The tongue speaks great things' (see Dan. 7, 8. And by the tongue is understood the foundation—namely, the letter I, *Yod*, joined with his bride; the speech is the marital influx flowing forth from the bride; for the queen is called the word; but the great things are the inferiors of all grades produced.)

The inferiors of all 'grades' or 'paths' are the Sephiroth in the inferior worlds.

This tongue is hidden between I, *Yod*, and H, *He*. (For father and mother are perpetually conjoined in ISVD, *Yesod*, the foundation, but concealed under the mystery of Daath or of knowledge.)

The conjunction of the letters V and H at the end of the Tetragrammaton IHVH is similar to that of I and H at the beginning.

Because it is written (Isa. 44, 5): 'That man shall say, I am of the Tetragrammaton.' (The word ANI, *Ani*, I, when the discourse is concerning judgments, pertains to the queen. But whenever mercy is introduced it refers to the understanding, like as in this place. In order that the sense may be: The supernal path, which is called I, or the understanding in act of conjunction with the father, is for the purpose of the formation of the Tetragrammaton, and this is one conjunction between the father and the mother for the constitution of the six members.) And that shall be called by the name Jacob, IOQB, *Yaqob*. (To call by name is to preserve; and another conjunction of father and mother is introduced for the purpose of preserving the Microprosopus, which is called Jacob.) And that man shall write with his hand, 'I am the Lord's.' (To write belongs to the written law, or the beautiful path, and the same also signifies to flow in. 'With his hand,' BIDV, *Byodo*, is by metathesis BIVD, *Byod*, by I, *Yod*—that is, through the foundation; in order that the sense may be, it may be formed from his influx, so that the Tetragrammaton may be written with I, *Yod*, as we have above said.) And by the name of Israel shall he call himself. He shall call himself thus in truth. (For the conception of the Microprosopus is more properly under the name of Jacob, whose wife is Rachel; and his cognomen, as it were, is Israel, whose wife is Leah.)

The understanding is Binan, the third Sephira, which is referred to the supernal H, *He*. The 'beautiful path' is Tiphereth, the sixth. The foundation is Yesod, the ninth. It is the *final* Yod, I, of the form of the Tetragrammaton IHVI, which is referred to Yesod, and not the initial, which belongs to Chokmah, the second Sephira, the Father.

That man shall say, I am the Lord's; he descends. (That is: that very conception of the word I, which is elsewhere attributed to the supernal mother, forasmuch as in her agree the three letters of the word ANI, *Ani*, I; namely A, *Aleph*, is the highest crown; N, *Nun*, is the understanding itself, in its fifty celebrated gates; I, *Yod*, is the foundation or knowledge of the Father; but in this instance it is attributed to the lowest grade of the lower mother, and now is ADNI, *Adonai*, without the D, *Daleth*, D, or poverty, but filled with the influx, and is ANI, *Ani*.) And all things are called BIDV, *Byodo* (that is, all these things are applied to IVD, *Yod*, concerning which this discourse is.) All things cohere by the tongue, which is concealed in the mother. (That is, through Daath, or knowledge, whereby wisdom is combined with the understanding, and the beautiful path with his bride the queen; and this is the concealed idea, or soul, pervading the whole emanation.) Since this is opened for that which proceeds from itself (that is, Daath is itself the beautiful path, but also the inner, whereto Moses refers; and that path lies hidden within the mother, and is the medium of its conjunction. But whenever it is considered in the outer, when it has come forth from the mother, then is it called Jacob.)

(And herein IHV *Yod, He, Vau* differs from the whole name and from all the four letters. Now, he turns back to the other portion of the four—namely, IHV, *Yod, He, Vau*—and says:) The Father resides in the beginning (that is, that the letter I, *Yod,* which is the symbol of the wisdom and of the father, in that part holds the first place, like as in the whole system; since the crown nevertheless is hidden, and is only compared to the highest apex of the letter I, *Yod*). The mother in the middle (for the letter H, *He,* which is the symbol of the unformed understanding and the supernal mother, holds the middle place between I, *Yod,* and V, *Vau,* even as in the supernals she is comprehended by the Father from above, and by the Microprosopus, which is her son, she is covered from below, in whom she sends herself downward into the path of Hod, or of glory.) And she is covered on this side and on that (by the two, father and son). Woe, woe unto him who reveals their nakedness! (Since this can be done by the faults of the inferiors, so that Microprosopus loses this influx, whereby he is of so great power that he can seek to enshroud his mother; for that covering is the reception of the supernal influx, and the capability of transmitting the same to the inferiors, which cannot be done if the mother be uncovered and taken away from the Microprosopus, as the Israelites did when they committed the sin of the calf.

IHV is of course the Tetragrammaton without the final H. It is interesting to note that in the kabalistical work called the *Sepher Yetzirah,* this trigrammatic name is used instead of the Tetragrammaton. The crown which is hidden is Kether, the first Sephira, or Macroprosopus, who is AHIH. and is therefore not openly shown in IHVH. The path of Hod is the eighth Sephira.

The father and the son, by whom the mother is enclosed, are of course the letters I and V in the word IHV. With regard to what is said regarding the Israelites when they committed the sin of the calf, I imagine that it is intended to intimate—(a) That the calf as a symbol of ALHIM, Elohim, not of IHVH; for the Israelites had said, 'Make us Elohim to go before us.' (b) That this name 'Elohim' is applied to the feminine portion of the Tetragrammaton HH. (c) That therefore the force was unbalanced which they adored, and that it would have been just as wrong to adore IV alone.

And God said, let there be MARTh, *Maroth*, lights in the firmament of the heaven. (Now he hastens to the third part of that quadrilateral name, namely, to these two letters IH, *Yod*, *He*. But by lights are understood the sun and the moon, the beautiful path and the kingdom or bride. And herein the sense is this: although usually by these two letters are accustomed to be understood the Father and the Mother, or the wisdom and the understanding, yet in this place the supernal lights are wanting, like as the word MARTh, *Maroth*, is written in a defective form; and the meaning is proper to be applied unto the firmament of the heaven—that is, to the foundation, extended and prepared for marital conjunction; for the spouse is called the heaven, and the member of the treaty is the firmament, like, as, therefore, the two last paths in the whole name IHVI, *Yod*, *He*, *Vau*, *Yod* are designated by the letters V, *Vau*, and I, *Yod*, so likewise these in this portion of the square are designated by the letters, I, *Yod*, and H, *He*.) The husband has dominion over the wife (since it is not written by V, *Vau*, but by I, *Yod*, which is the symbol of the member of the treaty, and herein denotes the actual combination with the female): like as it is written (Prov. 10, 25) 'And the just man is the foundation of the world.' (By this saying he illustrates his meaning; because by the letter I, *Yod*, is understood the fundamental member by which the world is preserved in existence.)

If the reader refers to the Introduction, he will there find on page 10), a diagram showing the operation of the Sephiroth in the four worlds, &c., that in the world of Asiah the sun is referred to Tiphereth and the moon to Yesod. Besides all these rules, there are certain meanings hidden in the shape of the letters of the Hebrew alphabet; in the form of a particular letter at the end of a word being different from that which it generally bears when it is a final letter, or in a letter being written in the middle of a word in a character generally used only at the end; in any letter or letters being written in a size smaller or larger than the rest of the manuscript, or in a letter being written upside down; in the variations found in the spelling of certain words, which have a letter more in some places than they have in others; in peculiarities observed in the position of any of the points or accents, and in certain expressions supposed to be elliptic or redundant. The term 'square,' or 'square name,' is sometimes applied to the Tetragrammaton. The phrase 'member of the treaty' probably alludes to the symbolism of circumcision. In this sense, I, *Yod*, in the path of Yesod, the ninth Sephira, has a symbolical phallic signification.

I, *Yod*, therefore irradiates two. (That is, the letter I, *Yod*, in this square of the Tetragrammaton has a double sense of influx, forasmuch as in the first instance it signifies the father who illuminates the mother; and forasmuch as in the second instance it signifies the Microprosopus, or rather his treaty, which illuminates the kingdom.) And (again in another manner) it shines (that is, and also has a third signification, whilst in the complete name it constitutes the last letter), and passes on into the woman. That is, and denotes the bride of Microprosopus, as is shown above, because it is put in the place of the last H, *He*, of the Tetragrammaton IHVH; like as also it has the same power of signification in the connection of the names of existence and domination in this manner, IAChD, VNHI.)

(Now he turns to the last part of this square, which is I, *Yod*, alone, and says), I, *Yod*, remains one and alone (in order that it may show that all flow out from the one sin-

gle letter I, *Yod*, which is in the form of a point, yet par-
taking of three parts, concerning which see elsewhere; yet
in this place denoting only the woman, or the kingdom,
wherein are contained all the supernals.)

> Yod at the end of the Tetragrammaton denotes the synthesis, the
> circular movement by which the end returns to the beginning. In
> the secret qabalistical alphabet known as the 'celestial alphabet,'
> Yod is represented by three circles at the angles of an equilateral
> triangle with the apex uppermost. Malkuth, the tenth Sephira, of
> course receives the influx of all the other Sephiroth (See diagram p
> 10 showing the reception and transmission of the Sephiroth in the
> four worlds.)

And then (if now the Tetragrammaton be not considered
in the manner just described, but in this manner of insti-
tuting the square, IHVI, IHV, IH, I, then *Yod* also is in a
certain sense solitary, but in a plainly contrary sense. For
it ascends in its path upwards and upwards. (That is, it
does not so much receive the *higher* sense, in order that it
may denote the beautiful path or the foundation; but the
highest, that is, the father or the wisdom.) The woman is
again hidden. (That is, in this instance, the former meaning by which it denoted the bride of Microprosopus,
namely, the last letter of the above-written form of the
Tetragrammaton, ceases in itself.)

> This is in the converse manner. The letter I no longer signifies the
> bride when it ceases to be the final letter of a Tetragrammaton.

And the mother is illuminated (that is, is the second part
of the ordinary averse Tetragrammaton, which consists of
the letters IH, to the letter I, *Yod*, which has the signification of the father, is added the letter H, *He*, which is the
mother, and because these two are combined by themselves, hence that luminous influence is denoted where-

with the understanding is imbued by the supernal wisdom); and is opened out into her gates (that is, if these two letters be bound closely together, then out of the dead the pentad originates the number 50, by which are denoted the fifty gates of the understanding; these are said to be opened because the letter H, *He*, is last and unprotected, not being shut in by any other succeeding letter.)

This is taking the letters IH separate from the rest of the Tetragrammaton, but themselves conjoined. And as I = 10 and H = 5, these two conjoined (multiplied together) give N = 50. And these are the fifty gates or properties of the understanding. These are opened, because in the word IH, *Yah*, the letter H is last, not being shut in, as by VH in the Tetragrammaton IHVH, or V in the trigram IHV.)

The key is added which contains six, and closes its gate. (That is, in the third part of this averse form, which is IHV, the letter H is not altogether the last; but V, the third letter of the Tetragrammaton, closes it in on the other side, whereby are denoted the six members of the Microprosopus, superinvesting the six members of the mother in such a manner that her last gate, which is the path of glory, HVD, *Hod*, is closed, and combined with the remainder, which are—Benignity, Severity, Beauty, Victory; drawing their existence singly out of the decad.)

In the Trigram IHV, V may be called the key, because it closes the fifty gates symbolized by IH, by coming neat to H, so as to close or shut in that letter between itself and I. By 'the decad' is meant the ten Sephiroth, which are symbolized by the numerical value of I, which is 10.

And it applies to the inferiors and to this part. (Or, as others read, 'it applies to this side and to that.' Now, the discourse is concerning the fourth part of the square, where the name is complete, whether written as H or as I in the last path; so that, nevertheless, the bride of Microprosopus may be added. Therefore on either side has Microprosopus a connecting link, for he superinvests the mother from the supernal part, so that he may receive her into himself as his soul; and he also again is covered by his bride from the inferior part, so that he in his turn may himself become her soul.)

> The bride, the inferior H, He, is said to be a reflection of the mother, the supernal H, *He,* in the Tetragrammaton; just as Microprosopus is said to be the reflection of Macroprosopus.

Woe unto him who shall open her gate! (The gates are said to be paths through which influence rushes forth; they are said to be closed, because, on the other hand, too much influence cannot be taken away from the inferiors; wherefore the members are said to be overshadowed by the members, so that the light may diminish in its transit. But when those very concatenations and cohibitions of the lights are separated by the sins of the inferiors, no influx can come into the universe in a proper manner.)

> Following out the symbol of the equilibrium in the Sephiroth, the sin of the inferior paths would be the introduction of unbalanced force. The reader will at first find a little difficulty in following the reasoning of these last few sections, but after reading them over once or twice, their meaning will seem clearer to him.

The six days of Creation as depicted in Coverdale's bible, the first printed version in English dating from the sixteenth century.

The beard of truth. (That is, now follows a description of the beard of Macroprosopus, and its thirteen parts, which are more fully described in the *Idra Rabba* or *The Greater Holy Assembly*.

The beard is the influx which descends from the first Sephira through all the others. Macroprosopus is the first Sephira, Kether, or the crown; also called the Ancient One.

Of the beard mention has not been made. (The correct Mantuan Codex has this correction, so that the word DQNA, *Deqena*, is here inserted in the original text. The meaning is, that Solomon in the *Song of Songs* makes mention of all the other members, but not of the beard.) Because this is the ornament of all. (It is called an ornament because it covers the rest, just as a garment which ornaments the body covers that. But this beard covers not only the Macroprosopus, but also the father and the mother, and descends even unto Microprosopus. Whence, on account of the communication of so copious a light, it has also itself been clothed as with a garment with the great reverence of silence.)

By this beard, covering 'not only Macroprosopus, but also the father and the mother,' is meant that, while it is an important attribute of Macroprosopus (who is, be it carefully remembered by the reader *Eheieh*, AHIH, and *not* IHVH, in which latter name he is only alluded to as 'the uppermost point of the letter I, *Yod*'), it also extends through the Sephiroth, for it covers the father and the mother (i.e., the second Sephira, *Chokinah*, wisdom, and the third Sephira, *Binah*, understanding, the IH of IHVH). Thus, therefore, though properly speaking a part of AHIH, and not of IHVH, it extends through the Tetragrammaton IHVH, for it 'descends even unto Microprosopus,' the next six Sephiroth, the six Sephiroth, the V of IHVH.

From the ears it proceeds about the circumference of the open space; the white locks ascend and descend. Into thirteen portions it is distributed in adornment. (Of all these see the explanation in the *Idra Rabba* or *The Greater Holy Assembly* and *Idra Zuta* or *The Lesser Holy Assembly*.)

Concerning that ornamentation it is written (Jer. 2, 6): 'No man passed through it; and where no man dwelt.' Man is without, man is not included therein; much less the male.

The verse runs in the English version 'Through a land that no man passed through, and where no man dwelt.'

Through thirteen springs are the fountains distributed (by which there is an influx upon Microprosopus and the inferiors). Four are separately joined together, but nine flow upon the body (or, as others read, by advice of the correct Mantuan Codex), encircle the garden (that is, the Microprosopus).

The four, separately joined, probably refer to the four letters of the Tetragrammaton. and the nine to the last nine Sephiroth—i.e., exclusive of Kether. The Garden, or Paradise, is another term expressive of the whole Sephirotic system in Atziloth, the archetypal world.

This ornamentation begins to be formed before the gate of the ears.

It descends in beauty into the beginning of the lips; from this beginning into that beginning.

There exists a path which goes out beneath the two galleries of the nostrils, in order that he may seek, to pass over transgression; like as it is written, Prov. 19, 11. 'And it is glory to pass over a transgression.'

> The parting of the moustache on the centre of the upper lip. 'It is his glory to pass over a transgression.'

Beneath the lips the beard goes into another beginning.

Beneath that another path goes forth.

It covers the approaches to the aromatic beginning which is above.

Two apples are beheld, to illuminate the lights.

> The two 'apples' or 'apple-trees,' are the cheeks. Compare with this the imagery of the Song of Solomon.

The influence of all flows down as far as the heart (therein hang suspended the superiors and the inferiors).

Among those locks which hang down, none shines forth above another.

The lesser cover the throat like an ornament; the greater are restored to perfect proportion.

The lips are free on every side. Blessed is he who shall become the receiver of their kisses.

In that influence of all stream down thirteen drops of most pure balm.

In this influence all things exist and are concealed.

At that time, when the seventh month draws nigh, those months shall be found to be thirteen (for in the Codex, so often said to be correct, this word ThRISR, *Tharisar*, or twelve, is expunged; as if it were then shown to be a year of thirteen months, according to the number of those thirteen divisions of the influence) in the supernal world, and the thirteen gates of mercy are opened. At that time (by which principally the day of expiation is meant, according to that passage of Isaiah 55, 6: 'Seek ye the Lord while He can be found.'

> The 'thirteen divisions of the influence in the supernal world' are of course these thirteen parts of the beard of Macroprosopus considered in the sense of Atziloth, the archetypal world, the habitation of the pure Sephiroth alone: 'Seek the Lord while he may be found.'

It is written, Gen. 1, 11: 'And the Lord said, Let the earth bring forth germination; (let there be) grass yielding seed.' (If here the word IHI, *Yehi*, 'let there be,' be inserted, they make nine words.) This is that which is written: 'And humble your bodies in the ninth of the month at even.' (This is to be understood concerning that time concerning which we have spoken above, because then the Lord is to be sought out.)

> VIAMR ALHIM ThDShA HARTz DShA OShB MZRIO ZRO, eight words, to which if IHI be added, we have nine. The English version = 'And God said, Let the earth bring forth grass, the herb yielding seed.'

(In that passage, Deut. 3, 24, where it is written): 'Adonai Jehovah, you have begun to show to your servant Your greatness,' the name, Tetragrammaton, IHVH exists perfectly written in its sides. (So that the name ADNI, *Adonai*, denotes the inferior H, *He*, from the one side; and the points of the name ALHIM, *Elohim*, denote the superior H, *He*, from the other side.)

> 'In its sides'—i.e., in its aspects. The points are the vowel marks.

But here in this progermination of the earth it is not perfect, because IHI, *Yehi* (let there be), is not written. (But
we read it so that also these letters do not represent a perfect name.)

(But therein is represented to us) the superior I, *Yod* (that
is, the mark of supernal mercy, which is that most holy
Ancient One, as the correct Mantuan Codex shows in a
marginal note), and the inferior I, *Yod* (that is, the mark of
inferior mercy, which is Microprosopus with the influence
which he has from Macroprosopus, which two II, *Yods*,
are also represented in that passage, Gen. 2, 7): VIITzR
IHVH, *Vayeyetsir*, *Yod*, *He*, *Vau*, *He*, and Tetragrammaton
formed the supernal I, *Yod*, (and the inferior I, *Yod*).

The only way that I can possibly see that VIITzR IHVH will bear
the construction put upon it here is this (in which an eminent
Hebrew scholar, Mr. Mew, agrees with me): V, Vau, and I, Yod, the
Yod, 1TzR, *Yetzer*, be formed (namely, the) IHVH,
Tetragrammaton. In this construction the first letter Yod in the
word VIITzR is taken as the object of the verb ITzR, and not as a
pronominal prefix. The most holy Ancient One is the origin of
Kether in Ain Soph when in the condition of the Ain Soph Aur
while the inferior Yod is the symbol of Yesod.

(But in) IHI (besides) the superior and inferior (also exists)
the H, *He*, between both (like as) a connexion of perfec-
tion (whereby the influx is derived from the
Macroprosopus and passed on to the Microprosopus.)

(Wherefore) it is perfect (since it is this name without
separation), but it is not turned to every side (because
therein is no symbol of the bride of Microprosopus).
(Therefore) this name is taken out from this place and
planted in another (that is, those letters also receive another signification from the inferior paths).

(For) it is written, Gen. 2, 8 'And the Tetragrammaton

Elohim planted.' (Whereby is understood) that H, *He*,
which is between the two II, *Yods*, of the word IHI, *Yehi*,
which in the supernals is) the position of the nose of the
more Ancient One over the Microprosopus. (For this)
exists not without the spirit.

> For this *H*, He, symbolised in Elohim, is rather the supernal *He*
> alone, than either the inferior *He* alone, or both conjoined. The
> nose of Macroprosopus is said in the *Idra Rabba* to be life in every
> part—i.e., it, the life, exists not therefore without the influx of the
> spirit which rushes forth therefrom .

Through H, *He*, therefore, it is perfected (rather by reason
of the mother than by reason of the bride, of whom it is
the soul). For the one H, *He*, is above (namely, designat-
ing the first understanding of the Tetragrammaton; and
the other is) the H, *He*, below (denoting the queen and the
bride).

Like as it is written, Jer. 32, 17 AHH ADNI IHVH,
Ahah, Adonai, Yod He Vau He: 'Ah, Lord Jehovah,' &c.,
where there is a cohesion of the connecting links (that is,
in the word AHH, *Ahah*, those two HH, *He's*, are combined which elsewhere are the media of the connecting
path). For by the spirit is made the connection of the balanced equilibria (that is, of the combinations as well of the
father and mother as of the Microprosopus and his bride).

(Now the author of the *The Book of Concealed Mystery*
descends to the inferior paths, leaving out
Macroprosopus, and examines the name IHV, *Yod He
Vau*. In this are represented father and mother and
Microprosopus. And first occurs) the supernal I, *Yod* (the
symbol of the father), which is crowned with the crown of
the more Ancient One (that is, whose highest apex denotes
the highest crown, or Macroprosopus; or, according to
another reading of the passage, 'which is surrounded by

the secret things'—that is by the influence or beard of Macroprosopus, which covers both the father and the mother). It is that membrane of the supernal brain which, on account of its excellency, both shines and is concealed.

The supernal H, *He* (then presents itself), which is surrounded by the spirit which rushes forth from the entrances of the galleries (or the nostrils of Macroprosopus), that it may give life to all things.

The supernal V, *Vau*, is that tremendous flashing flame (which is the beginning of judgment, seeing that doubtless hitherto the Microprosopus exists in the mother) which is surrounded by its crown (namely, the mother).

And after are the letters taken in extended form (so that this name is written at length, in this manner: VV, *Vau*, HH, *He*, IVD, *Yod*, which form, when it is perfect, is usually called BN, *Ben*, because its numeration is 52), and in Microprosopus are they comprehended (seeing that then he embraces his bride).

When (this form) begins, they are discovered in the cranium (namely, these letters, and therein are they distributed in the most supernal part of Macroprosopus).

'In the cranium' (or skull), BGVLGLThA, *Begolgoltha*, or in Golgoltha. In the New Testament it is worthy of note that Jesus Christ (the Son) is said to be crucified at Golgotha (the skull); while here, in the Qabalah, Microprosopus (the Son), as the Tetragrammaton, is said to be extended in the form of a cross, thus—

I

H   H

V

—in Golgotha (the skull). The text above says, 'of Macroprosopus'; but I think this is a misprint for 'of Microprosopus.'

Thence are they extended throughout his whole form (from the original benignity), even to the foundation of all things (namely, as the soul of the inferiors).

When it is balanced in the pure equilibrium (that is, when the white locks of the most holy Ancient One send down the lights or names) then are those letters equilibrated. (That is, from their virtue comes the light.)

The 'lights or names' are the ten Sephiroth and the Divine names associated with them which are (with the exception of the first Sephira) comprehended in the Tetragrammaton IHVH.

When he is manifested in Microprosopus (namely, Macroprosopus), in him are those letters, and by them is he named.

IVD, *Yod*, of the Ancient One, is hidden in its origin (that is, the father, who is usually symbolized by I, *Yod*, and is himself also called the Ancient One, is shrouded by the beard of Macroprosopus; or otherwise. Instead of that manner in which the other two letters duplicate their literal parts—*e.g.*, HH and VV—I, *Yod*, by reason of his very nature, cannot be expressed by this duplication, but remains one and alone), because the name is not found; that is, because if II be put, it can no longer be pronounced as I, *Yod*; therefore is it written IVD).

The 'Ancient One' is one of the titles of Macroprosopus, the first Sephira. But the letter I, *Yod*, of the Tetragrammaton is referred to the second Sephira. Chokmah, which is also called the Father.

HA, *He*, is extended by another *(He*, as it is written HH in open and plain writing; but also it is sometimes written in another way, HI, also HA; the one in the name OB, *Aub*, the other in the name MH, *Mah*), and in the feminine symbol it denotes the two females (namely, the supernal mother and the inferior mother; the understanding and the kingdom). And it is discovered through the forms. (That is, when the beard of Macroprosopus, and its forms or parts, send down his light into Microprosopus; then herein is his bride produced in the light, and the supernal H, *He*, is reflected by another inferior H, *He*.)

See Diagram p.10.

VV, *Vau*, is extended by another *(Vau*, as it is written VV, for likewise it is elsewhere written with I in the name OB, *Aub*, and by A in the names SG, *Seg*, and MH, *Mah*, in this manner VAV. So also in the name BN, *Ben*, it is thus written, VV. But to be disclosed it is fully written). Like as it is written, Cant. 7, 9, 'Going down sweetly to my delight' (whereby 'sweetly' are understood these two letters VV properly extended).

> The Authorised Version renders it: 'And the roof of your mouth like the best wine for my beloved, that goes down sweetly, causing the lips of those that are asleep to speak.'

In that tremendous flashing flame (is he found—*i.e.*, in Microprosopus, seeing that in a lesser degree he has in himself unmixed judgments), for the purpose of enshrouding that gate (that is, in order that he may be advanced to the condition of maturity, and may then superumbrate his mother, who is symbolised by the fifty gates).

> 'He,' that is the letter V, *Vau*, of the Tetragrammaton. I have before noticed that the fifty gates of the understanding are equivalent to I and H, 10 and 5, multiplied together, which yield 50 = numerical value of the letter N, *Nun*.

(He is therefore called) the supernal V, *Vau* (Daath or

knowledge, and) the inferior V, *Vau* (that is, the external Microprosopus. And thus also) the supernal H, *He* (the mother), the inferior H, *He* (the bride). But I, *Yod*, is above all (symbolizing the father), and with him is none other associated; he is I, *Yod*, as at first; neither ascends he in himself (through the height of the numeration, like as with H, *H*, the pentad, with *Vau*, the hexad, ascend to a similar height) except as a symbolic glyph. (That is, the decad, which is expressed not in that same letter I, *Yod*, but by a hexad and a tetrad).

But Vau, V, is produced by *adding* the numerical values of I and H (the father and the mother of the Tetragrammaton), and then taking the least number of the result, thus; I + H = 10 + 5 = 15, and by adding the digits of 15 together, 1 + 5, we obtain 6 = V, *Vau*. By the phrase 'with H, *He*, the pentad (5), with V, *Vau*, the hexad (6), ascend,' is implied the numerical value of those *letters taken as symbolical sephirotic glyphs*. The decad is repeated in the word IVD, *Yod*, by the addition of the last two letters, V and D, which = 6 + 4 = 10, I, *Yod*, again.

For when the double forms are manifested (namely, the letters of the name in the above proposed form, as HH and VV) and are united in one path, in one combination, in order that they may be explained (that is, when they are fully written out in the above manner), then VD, *Vau*, *Daleth* (and *not* another I, *Yod*), are added to I, *Yod* (so that also in it there may be a certain hidden analogy of the equilibrium).

Woe! woe! when this is taken away, and when the other two alone are manifested (that is, when from those two letters VD, in the word IVD, the letter I is taken away; seeing it represents the abstraction of the father from the Microprosopus and his bride, who are as yet hidden in the mother, so that the disclosure of these two is vain and abortive, because the generative power of the father is absent). (Or, in another sense, if the influx be 'hindered and the supernal paths suffer disruption). Far, far from us be that effect!

(But that this may be done by the sins of the inferiors is clear from these words) Ezek. 1, 14: 'And the living creatures rush forth and return.' Also Num. 24, 11: 'Flee to you place.' Also Obad. 1, 4: 'Though you exalt yourself as the eagle, and though you set your nest among the stars, thence will I cast you down.'

(Again it is said) Gen. 1, 12: 'And the earth brought forth germination.' When? When the name is planted therein.

And then the wind blows (that is, the vital influx rushes forth from Macroprosopus) and the spark of flame is prepared (that is, Microprosopus, who, great as he is, yet is in respect of the superiors only as a spark compared with fire, as he is produced from that terrific light.)

And amid the insupportable brilliance of that mighty light, as it were, the likeness of a head appears. (That is, the highest crown is found in Macroprosopus.)

And above him is the plenteous dew, diverse with two-fold colour. (Like as in Macroprosopus it is white alone, so here it is white and red, on account of the judgments.)

Above Microprosopus, not Macroprosopus.

Three hollow places are manifested, wherein the letters are expressed. (These are to be understood as symbolizing his three-fold brain, of wisdom, understanding, and knowledge, which here appear more plainly; whereas in the supernals they are more concealed.)

'The letters,' that is, IHV, the first three letters of the Tetragrammaton.

The black (locks issuing) from the four (sides of the head)

float down over the curved openings of the ears, so that he may *not* hear.

'So that he may not hear.' Remember, this is Microprosopus, or Zauir Anpin, not Macroprosopus, or Arikh Anpin.

Right and left is here given (in all parts of the face and head).

'Right and left:' that is, Microprosopus is symbolized by a face in full; while in Macroprosopus 'all is right'—i.e., he is symbolized by a profile.

One slender higher path exists. (The parting of the hair.)

His forehead, which shines not, regulating the far distant future when it is his will to behold the same.

His eyes are of triple colour (that is, red, black and gold) so that terror may go before them; and with glittering glory are they glazed.

It is written, Isa. 33, 20: 'Your eyes shall behold Jerusalem at peace, even your habitation.'

Also it is written, Isa. 1, 21: 'Righteousness dwelled in it.'

The 'peaceful habitation' is the Ancient One, who is hidden and concealed. Wherefore 'your eyes' is written OINK, *Auinak* (without the letter *Yod*.)

There is also the nose, to dignify the face of Microprosopus.

Through its nostrils three flames rush forth.

The profound path exists in his ears for hearing both the good and the evil.

(It is written, Isa. 42, 8: 'I am the Tetragrammaton, that is my name, and my glory I give not to another.' (Now the author of *The Book of Concealed Mystery* begins to explain the ulterior difference between Microprosopus and Macroprosopus, even as to their appellations; where the word ANI, *Ani*, 'I,' in the above passage refers to the Microprosopus, since it involves the idea of the bride.) Also it is written, Deut. 32, 39: 'I slay, and I make alive.' Also it is written, Isa. 46, 4 : 'I will bear, and I will deliver you.'

> In the word ANI, *Ani*, the idea of the bride (Malkuth, the H final of the Tetragrammaton) is implied by the letter I, *Yod*, being last, where it symbolizes the ninth Sephira, *Yesod*, which is the connecting link between Microprosopus and the queen. Also N, the second letter, symbolizes the conjunction of the father and the mother, I and H, as I have before observed.

Now, indeed, Macroprosopus is not so closely known by us as to address us in the first person; but he is called in the third person, HVA, *Hoa*, he.) Like as it is said, Ps. 100, 3: '*He* has made us, and not we ourselves.' And again in Job 23, 13: 'And *He* exists in the unity, and who can turn *Him* aside?'

> For Macroprosopus is only the commencement of manifested Deity.

(Therefore in the third person, HVA, *Hoa*, is He called who is the Concealed One, and is not found of any. He, who comes not before the eyes of man; He, who is not called by the Name.

> He, who is not called by the Name;' for, as I have frequently before noticed, the first Sephira is not comprehended in the Tetragrammaton.

(Hitherto has the disquisition been concerning Microprosopus, to whom also was referred that fulness of form of the letter H, *He*, wherein it is written by the duplicated HH. But now another point is taken into consideration, namely, concerning the remaining two modes of writing that letter, when It is written with A, *Aleph*, and with I, *Yod*; of which the former is made in the name MH, *Mah*, and the latter in the names OB, *Aub*, and SG, *Seg*; which two forms are given conjoined in the name AHIH, *Eheieh* (translated 'I am' in Exodus). Therefore are to be considered) HA and HI. (Whilst, therefore, it is written HA, this form can be resolved into HVA, *Hoa*, he, that pronoun of the third person concerning which mention has been made above: because A, *Aleph*, in itself contains V, *Vau*; to which latter letter the middle line, in the form of the character of the letter *Aleph*, can be assimilated. And thus, while it is written HA, the word HVA can be symbolized; but not *vice versa*. For although V in itself contains A (because the figure of the letter A may be said to be composed of VIV, if its middle line be divided; so that also, without taking the whole character A into consideration, it may be read HV: this HV) nevertheless does not contain in itself any real form of writing H, so that it can be read HV or HI.

> The reader must remember that the argument in this section is concerning the shape of the Hebrew letters mentioned, alone, and that neither their numerical value nor articulate power is taken into consideration. The shape of the Hebrew letters can be seen in the Table of the Alphabet p.12.

(Moreover, in that same form of writing HA, like as A passes into V, so that HVA, *Hoa*, may be read: so also) A is pronounced *Aleph* (and this is the second way of pronouncing the writing HA, which simply is referred to MH, *Mah*. But, moreover, also) Aleph is pronounced as IVD, *Yod* (because the form of the letter A is usually resolved into these three letters, so that *Yod* may be above, *Vau* in the middle, and *Daleth* below. So that same written form

HA in itself comprehends also that sublimer triune idea. But not *vice versa*, from HI is HA to be understood, for I, *Yod*, is not pronounced Aleph; but IVD is pronounced as I, *Yod*, which is concealed with all concealments, and to which VD are not joined (like as that form is to be found in the shape of the letter *Aleph*.)

> H, *He*, in Hebrew is the definite article; so that H-A may be read He-Aleph, the Aleph.

(But this form, which in itself includes V, *Vau*, and D, *Daleth*, is usual in the inferior paths, and also in the father. And) Woe! when I, *Yod*, irradiates not the letters V, *Vau*, and D, *Daleth*; (and much more) when I, *Yod*, is taken away from V, *Vau*, D, *Daleth*, through the sins of the world; (because then) the nakedness of them all is discovered.

Therefore it is written, Lev. 18, 7: 'The nakedness of your father you shall not uncover.' (For VD, *Vau Daleth* are the same as H, *He*; and when it is written IVD, it is the same as if it were called IH (namely if V, *Vau*, be inserted in D, *Daleth*). Woe! when *Yod* is taken away from *He* (that is, wisdom from understanding, which is the conceiving mother) because it is written, Lev. 18, 7: 'And the nakedness of your mother you shall not uncover; she is your mother, you shall not uncover her nakedness.' Revere her; she is your mother; because it is written, Prov. 2, 3: 'Because you shall call understanding your mother.'

Moses and the Burning Bush. An engraving from an eighteenth-century edition of the Bible.

Nine are said to be the conformations of the beard (of Microprosopus). For that which remains concealed (that is, the other four forms, which meanwhile are not found in Microprosopus), and which is not manifested, is supernal and venerable (that is, properly and of itself does not refer to Microprosopus, but nevertheless descends upon him in another manner).

> It must be remembered that the beard of Macroprosopus had thirteen divisions, therefore the other four forms are the difference between the nine of Microprosopus and the thirteen of Macroprosopus.

Thus, therefore, is this most excellent beard arranged. The hairs overhang the hairs from before the opening of the ears, even to the beginning of the mouth. (This is the first conformation.)

From the one beginning even to the other beginning (of the mouth. This is the second conformation—namely, the beard on the upper lip).

Beneath the two nostrils exists a path filled with hairs, so that it does not appear. (This is the third conformation.)

The cheeks extend on one side and on the other. (This is the fourth conformation.)

In them appear apples red as roses. (This is the fifth conformation.)

In one tress hang down those hairs strong and black,

even to the breast. (This is the sixth conformation.)

Red are the lips as roses, and bare. This is the seventh conformation.)

Short hairs descend through the place of the throat and cover the position of the neck. (This is the eighth conformation.)

Long and short descend alike. (This is the ninth conformation.)

Whosoever is found among them, is found strong and robust. (That is, he who directs his meditations herein.)

It is written, Ps. 118, 4: 'I called upon Yah, IH, in distress.' (In this place) David commemorates (these) nine (conformations) even unto (those words) 'all nations compassed me about,' in order that they (the nine above mentioned) might surround and protect him.

(It is written, Gen. 1, 12): 'And the earth brought forth germination, the herb yielding seed after its kind; and the tree bearing fruit, whose seed is therein, according to its kind.'

Those nine (paths of Microprosopus) are evolved from the perfect name (that is, from the understanding or mother, in whom they were conceived; for to her pertains the name IHVH, which is Tetragrammaton expressed and Elohim hidden, which form the nine in power). And thence are they planted into the perfect name, like as it is written, Gen. 2, 8: 'And IHVH ALHIM planted' (that is, these nine letters of the perfect masculine and feminine name, so that they may be a garden—that is, Microprosopus in action).

By the expression 'Tetragrammaton expressed and Elohim hidden,' is meant that the former is written with the vowel points of the latter. They 'form nine in power,' because the four letters IHVH together with the five letters ALHIM make nine.

The conformations of the beard (of Microprosopus) are found to be thirteen when that which is superior becomes inferior. (That is, whenever the beard of Macroprosopus sends down its light. But in the inferior (that is, Microprosopus taken by himself), they are beheld in nine (parts of that form).

The twenty-two letters are figured forth in their colour; not only when the law is given forth in black fire upon white fire, but also in ordinary writings, because this beard is black.

> The number of the letters of the Hebrew alphabet is twenty-two. 'Black fire' and 'white fire' are the colours of the beards of Microprosopus and of Macroprosopus respectively.)

Concerning this (beard, that is understood which is said) concerning him who in his sleep beholds the beard. 'When any one dreams that he takes the upper beard of a man in his hand, he has peace with his Lord, and his enemies are subject to him.'

By the 'upper beard' is meant the moustache.

Much more (if he seeks to touch) the supernal beard. For the inferior light, taking its rise from the supernal light which exists within the benignity (thus the beard of Macroprosopus is entitled), is called in Microprosopus the benignity in a more simple manner; but when it has its action within the light, and it shines; then is it called abounding in benignity. (Others read this passage thus:— He who dreams that he touches the moustache of a man with his hand, he may be sure that be has peace with his Lord, and that his enemies are subject unto him. If that happens because he beholds in sleep such a thing as this only, much more shall it occur if he be found sufficiently worthy to behold what the supernal beard may he. For this, seeing that it is the superior, and is called the benignity, irradiates the inferior. But in Microprosopus, &c.)

It is written, Gen. 1, 20: 'Let the waters bring forth the reptile of a living soul' (Ch-IH, *Chiah*, living creature is to be here noted).

(To this section belongs the annotation which is placed at the end of this chapter p.63.)

Like as it is said IH, *Yah* (Ch-IH, *Ch-iah*, the corrected Mantuan Codex has it, so that it may explain the word ChIH, *Chiah*, living creature, out of the eighth path of the understanding, which is that water of the name *Yah*, which denotes father and mother. For when) the light of the former is extended to the latter (which is the moving of the water) all things reproduce their kind at one and the same time—the waters of good and the waters of evil. (That is, there is reproduction as well in divinity and sanctity as among terrestrial living creatures and man; for by the reptile form souls are symbolized.)

(For) while it says: IShRTzV, *Yeshratzu*, 'Let them bring forth abundantly,' they have vital motion; and the one form is at once included in the other form; the living superior, the living inferior; the living good, the living evil.

(So also it is written, Gen. 1, 26): 'And Elohim said, Let us make man.' (Where) it is not written HADM, *Ha-Adam*, 'this man'; but *Adam*, man, simply, in antithesis of the Higher One who has been made in the perfect name.

When that one was perfected, this one also was perfected; but perfected as male and female, for the perfecting of all things.

(When therefore it is said) IHVH, *Yod, He, Vau, He* (then is expressed), the nature of the male. (When) ALHIM, *Elohim* (is joined therewith, there is expressed), the nature of the female (who is called the kingdom).

'The female who is called the kingdom,' i.e., Malkuth, the tenth Sephira.

(Therefore) was the male extended, and formed with his members (in order that he might have), as it were, regenerative power.

> The 'members of the male' are the six Sephiroth which together form Microprosopus.

By means of this regenerative power those kings, who had been destroyed, were herein restored, and obtained stability. (For when the lights were sent down through narrow channels in less abundance, the inferior intelligences could take possession of them.)

> The 'kings who had been destroyed' are the 'Edomite kings,' the 'worlds of unbalanced force,' who could not subsist because the 'form of the heavenly man' was not as yet.

The rigours (of judgments, which are symbolized by those kings), which are masculine, are vehement in the beginning; but in the end they are slackened. In the female the contrary rule obtains.

(We have an example of this in this form of the name) VIH (where the male has two letters, and the female one only; and the masculine also the letter in the beginning long, and afterwards short. But also in this form) the channels of connection are shrouded beneath His covering (that his, the supernal letters are doubtless connected in marital conjunction, but they are enshrouded in the letter *Vau*. And) *Yod* (is in this place) small, (a symbol of the foundation; because) in the very form (of the female, that is, even as he is hidden within H, *He*, which also is not the supernal but the inferior H, *He*) he is found. (And all are judgments, because the supernal influx is wanting.)

But if (these) judgments are to be mitigated, necessarily

the Ancient One is required (that is, the first letters of the Tetragrammaton, denoting, IH *Yah*, the father together with the crown, which is the apex of the primal letter, and is called Macroprosopus.)

The same species of rigours and judgments occurred in the inferiors. For like as to the *He* of the bride, are added the two letters *Yod* and *Vau*, under the idea of the leviathan; (so) the serpent came upon the woman, and formed in her a nucleus of impurity, in order that he might make the habitation evil.

Like as it is written, Gen. 4, 1: 'And she conceived and brought forth ATh QIN, *Ath Qain*, Cain, (that is) the nucleus QINA, *Qaina*, of the abode of evil spirits, and turbulence, and evil occurrences.'

(But this name VIH) is restored (if it be written IHV; and thus) in that man (the supernal, concerning whom it has been spoken above; and also) in those two (namely, the father and the mother, also in the androgynous Microprosopus; and also partly) in genus (seeing that *Vau* alone symbolizes both the Microprosopus and his bride) and in species (seeing that *Yod* and *He* are placed separately as father and mother).

(But just as much) are they contained in the special (representation of those spouses, as) also in the general (that is, as much in father and mother as in Microprosopus with his bride); legs and arms right and left (that is, the remaining numerations, collected together in two lateral lines, with the middle line representing Vau and *Yod*.)

(But) this (that is, the supreme equality) is divided in its sides, because *Yod* and *He* are placed expressly as the father and the mother; but in another equality) the male is conformed with the female (like an androgyn, because the last *He* is not added. Whence are made) IHV.

I, *Yod*, is male (namely, the father); H, *He*, is female

(namely, the mother); V, *Vau* (however, is androgynous, like as) it is written, Gen. 5, 2: 'Male and female created He them, and blessed them, and called their name Adam.'

(Thus also) the form and person of a man was seated upon the throne; and it is written, Ezek. 1, 26: 'And upon the likeness of the throne was the likeness as the appearance of a man above it.'

This piece alludes to the Tetragrammaton itself, showing the hieroglyphic form of a man: the I = head, H = arms, V = body, and H = legs. See the Table of Alphabet p.12.

ANNOTATION
(See p.60)
Another explanation. 'Let waters bring forth abundantly.' In this place, in the Chaldee paraphrase, it is said IRChShVN, which has a general meaning of movement. As if it should be said : 'When his lips by moving themselves and murmuring, produced the words, like a prayer from a righteous heart and pure mind, the water produced the living soul.' (The meaning is concerning the act of generating life.)

And when a man wishes to utter his prayers rightly before the Lord, and his lips move themselves in this manner, (his invocations) rising upward from him, for the purpose of magnifying the majesty of his Lord to the place of abundance of the water where the depth of that fountain rises and flows forth (that is, understanding emanating from wisdom); then (that fountain flows forth plentifully, and) spreads abroad so as to send down the influx from the Highest, downwards from that place of abundance of water, into the paths singly and conjointly, even to the last path; in order that her bountiful grace may be derived into all from the highest downwards.

H, *He,* the supernal mother.

Then indeed is such a man held to intertwine the connecting links of (them) all, namely, those connecting links of true and righteous meditation; and all his petitions shall come to pass, whether his petition be made in a place of worship, whether in private prayer.

'Such a man'—i.e., a righteous man, when praying sincerely. 'Links of them'—i.e., the paths.

But the petition, which a man wishes to make to his Lord can ordinarily be propounded in nine ways.

Either (1) by the alphabet, or (2) by commemorating the attributes of the most holy and blessed God, merciful and gracious, &c. (according to the passage in Exodus 34, 6, &c.); or (3) by the venerable names of the most holy and blessed God; such are these: AHIH, *Eheieh* (in respect of the Crown), and IH, *Yah* (in respect of the Wisdom); IHV, *Yod He Vau* (in respect of the Understanding); AL, *El* (in respect of the Majesty); ALHIM, *Elohim* (in respect of the Severity); IHVH, *Yod He Vau He* (in respect of the Beauty); TzBAVTh, *Tzabaoth* (in respect of the Victory and the Glory) ShDI, *Shaddai* (in respect of the Foundation); and ADNI, *Adonaï* (in respect of the Kingdom). Or (4) by the ten Sephiroth or numerations, which are: MLKVTh, *Malkuth,* the Kingdom; ISVD, *Yesod,* the Foundation; HVD, *Hod,* the Glory; NTzCh, *Netzach,* the Victory; ThPARTh, *Tiphereth,* the Beauty; GBVRH, *Geburah,* the Severity; ChSD, *Chesed,* the Benignity; BINH, *Binah,* the Understanding; ChKMH, *Chokhmah,* the Wisdom; and KThR, *Kether,* the Crown. Or (5) by the commemoration of just men, such as are patriarchs, prophets, and kings. Or (6) by those canticles and psalms wherein is the true Qabalah. And (7), above all these, if any one should know how to declare the conformations of his Lord, according as it is honourable to do. Or (8) if he may know how to ascend from that which is below to that which is above. Or (9) those who know also how to derive the influx from the highest downward. And in all these nine ways there is need of very great concentration of attention because if he does not that, it is written concerning him, 1 Sam. 2, 30: 'And they that despise Me shall be lightly esteemed.'

(1) 'by the alphabet'—i.e., according to the mystic qabalistico, theosophic values of the letters. (2) Exod. 34, 6, 7: 'And the Lord passed by before him, and proclaimed, The Lord, the Lord God, merciful and gracious, long-suffering and abundant, in goodness and truth, keeping mercy for thousands, forgiving iniquity and transgression and sin, and that will by no means clear the guilty: visiting the iniquity of the fathers upon the children, and upon the children's children, to the third and to the fourth generation.' (3) By the Divine Names associated with the Sephiroth. (4) The ten Sephiroth. (5) Those analogous to his desire. (6) Phrases bearing on the subject. (7) The qabalistical development of Deity. (8) By the paths. (9) The converse of (8).

Hereto also pertains the meditation of the word *Amen* AMN! which in itself contains the two names IHVH, ADNI, *Yod He Vau He Adonai* (the numeration of the former alone, and of these two together yielding the same, 91); of which the one conceals its goodness and benediction in that treasury which is called HIKL, *Ha-yekal*, the palace. (Which word by equality of numeration is the same as ADNI, *Adonaï*; but this name is said to be the palace of Tetragrammaton, because, in the first place it is pronounced by its aid; also, in the second place, it is mingled with it alternately, letter by letter, in this way— IAHDVNHI.

A + M + N = 1 + 40 + 50 = 91. I + H + V + H + A + D + N + I = 10 + 5 + 6 + 5 + 1 + 4 + 50 + 10 = 91. Again: H + I + K + L = 5 + 10 + 20 + 30 = 65. A + D + N + I = 1 + 4 + 50 + 10 = 65. The Jews, when they come to the word IHVH in reading the Scriptures, either do not pronounce it at all and make a slight pause, or else substitute for it the word Adonaï, ADNI.

And this is pointed out in that saying, Hab. 2, 20: 'But the Lord is in His holy temple; let all the earth keep silence before Him.' (HIKL, *Ha-yekal*, 'the temple, or palace;' HS, *Hes*, 'keep silence; 'and ADNI, *Adonaï*, 'Lord;' all have the same numeration—namely, 65.)

H + S = 5 + 6 = 65.

For which reason our wise men of pious memory have said mystically, that every good thing of a man is in his house; according to that which is written, Num. 11, 7: 'He is faithful in all Mine house.' Which is the same as if it were said 'in all which is with Me.'

But if any man attentively meditates on the nine divisions of these forms like as it is meet to do; that man is one who honours the Name of his Lord, even the Holy Name. And here belongs that which is written, 1 Sam. 2, 30: 'Since those who honour Me will I honour; and they that despise Me shall be lightly esteemed.' I will honour him in this world, that I may preserve him, and provide him with all things of which he has need, in order that all nations of the earth may see that the Name of the Lord is called upon by him; and that they may fear him. And in the world to come he shall be found worthy to stand in the tabernacle of the righteous.

Wherefore such a one seeks nothing of which he has need, because he is kept under the special providence of his Lord, and can meditate concerning Him, as it is right to do.

But what is to be understood by that passage—'And they that despise Me shall be lightly esteemed?' Such a one is that man who can neither institute the union of the Holy Name, nor bind together the links of truth, nor derive the supernals into the position required, nor honour the Name of his Lord. Better were it for that man had he never been created, and much more for that man who does not attentively meditate when he says Amen!

For which reason, concerning that man especially who moves his lips (in prayer), with a pure heart (meditating) on those purifying waters, in that passage expressly and clearly written, Gen. 1, 26; 'And the Elohim said, Let us make man.' As if it were said concerning such a man who knew how to unite image and likeness, as it is right: 'And they shall have dominion over the fish of the sea, &c.'

Adam and Eve take the apple offered by the serpent.
An engraving by Albrecht Dürer dating from 1511.

CHAPTER 4

The Ancient One is hidden and concealed; the Microprosopus is manifested, and is not manifested.

The 'Ancient One' is Kether, Eheieh, Macroprosopus, the Vast Countenance.

When he is manifested, he is symbolized by the letters (in the ordinary form in which the Tetragrammaton is written).

When he is concealed, he is hidden by the letters which are not disposed according (to the proper order) of the letters, or (according to another reading of this passage) in their proper place; because also in him their superiors and inferiors are not rightly disposed (because of the disturbed transpositions).

In Gen. 1, 24 it is written: 'The earth brought forth the living creature after its kind, cattle and reptile,' &c. Here belongs that which is written, Ps. 35, 7: 'O Lord, you shall preserve both man and beast.'

The one is contained under the general meaning of the other, and also the beast under the general idea of the man (on account of the mystery of the revolution of the soul).

(And here pertains that passage) Levit. 1, 2: 'When a

man shall bring *from among you* an offering to the Lord, &c. You shall offer, &c.' Because animals are included under the generic term man.

When the inferior man descends (into this world), like to the supernal form (in himself), there are found two spirits. (So that) man is formed from two sides—from the right and from the left.

With respect to the right side he had NShMThA QDIShA, *Neschamotha Qadisha*, the holy intelligences; with respect to the left side, NPSh ChIH, *Nephesh Chiah*, the animal soul.

Man sinned and was expanded on the left side and then they who are formless were expanded also. (That is those spirits of matter, who received dominion in the inferior paths of the soul of Adam, from where arose base concupiscence.) When (therefore) both were at once joined together (namely by base concupiscence, together with connexion, and the animal soul) generations took place, like as from some animal which generates many lives in one connexion.

(There are given) twenty-two letters hidden and twenty-two letters manifested (which are the symbols of those sublime forms).

(The one) *Yod* is concealed; the other is manifested. (The one is the understanding or mother, the other is the kingdom or queen; so that at the same time it looks back to the superior paths.) But that which is hidden and that which is manifest are balanced in the equilibrium of forms. (That is, masculine and feminine; the one, the father and the mother; the other, the foundation and the queen; meaning principally the female idea, which includes form and receptacle.)

Out of *Yod* are produced male and female (if, namely, it be fully written as IVD, *Yod*, they are then its augment),

Vau and *Daleth*. In this position *Vau* is male, and *Daleth* is female. And hence arise DV, the two letters which are the duad male and female; and not only the duad, but also the co-equal duads (of the superior and inferior conjunctions).

Yod by itself is male (the father); *He*, female (the mother).

H, *He*, at first was D, *Daleth*; but after it was impregnated by I, *Yod* (so that thence it might produce the form H—namely the I, *Yod*, placed at the left hand lower part of *Daleth*) it brought forth V, *Vau*. (That is, the mother impregnated by the father produced Microprosopus. But in the shape of the letter out of that minute I, *Yod*, which is hidden within the H, *He*, V, *Vau*, is said to be formed. Or from the upper horizontal line of the letter H, which is one V, *Vau*, and from the right-hand vertical line, which is another V, *Vau*, and from the inserted I, *Yod*, is made VIV, the full form of letter *Vau*.)

This is again referring to the shape of the letter. See Table of the Alphabet for Hebrew form p.12.

From where it is plain that in the letter H, *He*, are hidden the letters D, *Daleth*, V, *Vau*; and in IVD, *Yod*, is hidden H: whence are formed IHV. Therefore it appears that IVD in its own form contains IHV, whenever it is fully written by IVD, which are male and female (namely I, *Yod*, male, and V, V*au*, D, *Daleth*, in the form, H, *He*, female); hence is compounded (the son, who is) V, *Vau*, and who overshadows his mother. (That is V placed after H, so that IHV may form the father, the mother, and Microprosopus.)

(Therefore in the letter IVD, *Yod*, and in the name IHI are hidden two males and two females, which is symbolized in that saying, Gen. 6, 2: 'And the sons of the Elohim beheld (the plural in its least form denotes two) the daughters of men' (and this also). This explains on this account that which is written, Josh. 2, 1: 'Two men as spies, saying' (hence is revealed the mystery of the two men). But how (is it proved that two females are understood) by the words, 'Daughters of men?' Because it is written, 1 Kings 3, 16: 'Then came there two women to the king.'

Of these it is written: 'Because they saw that the wisdom of Elohim was in him.' (Here are involved the two males, in the wisdom, the father; in Solomon, Microprosopus. Therefore) then came they (even the two women, the understanding and the queen) and not before.

In the palace of the union of the fountains (that is, in the world of creation) there were two connexions by conjunctions among the supernals; these descended from above, and occupied the earth; but they rejected the good part, which in them was the crown of mercy; and were crowned with the cluster of grapes. (That is instead of benignity, they were surrounded with judgments and rigours. Which also can be explained concerning Microprosopus and his bride, first in the mother, and afterwards in the existences below, and in exile with surrounding rigours and severties.)

Referring to the previous symbolical explanation of Joshua 2, 1.

(Also we find these two equations in that saying) Exod. 14, 15 'And the Lord said to Moses (who is referred to the mother), Why do you cry to Me?' (But also a cry is referred to the mother, just as a groan is to the beautiful path, and an exclamation to the kingdom. But) ALI, *Eli*, to me (note this is the same as, 'and to I, *Yod*; 'or the father). 'Speak to the children of Israel (the speech is the queen; Israel is the beautiful path) that they set forward.' Wherein note well the word VISOV, *Vayesaau*, 'that they set forward,' wherein are VI masculine letters; SO feminine letters).

'But also a cry, &c.' Meaning the three Sephiroth, *Binah*, *Tiphereth*, and *Malkuth*.

From above the power of life flowed down in equilibrium, for he entreated the influence of the Venerable One.

Here also pertains that passage, Exod. 15, 26: 'And if you shall do right in His eyes, and shall listen to His precepts, and shall keep all His statutes.' (Where in the last word also two equations are placed.) 'Because I am the Lord your God who heals you.' (Note this, because again here is hidden the mystery of the understanding and the wisdom, of the path of beauty and of the congregation of Israel.)

Ezekiel's vision of the chariot drawn by cherubin.
A seventeenth-century engraving.

CHAPTER 5

I t is written in Isa. 1, 4: 'Woe to the sinful nation, to the people heavy with iniquity, to the seed of evildoers, &c' (Here the author of *The Book of Concealed Mystery* reasons concerning the small word HVI, 'woe,' which also is a form of the name. And this word is alone separated from the following portions of the sentence.)

Seven are the paths (if the Tetragrammaton be written in this way partially complete), IVD, HH, V, H, (where the father and mother are written in full, Microprosopus and his bride are written uncovered. If here the last and first letters be combined, and the penultimate and second, and therefore the paths at either extremity, so that they may form the letters) HI and VV (mother and son), then are produced (the three middle letters) HH, D (which are the symbols of the queen, heavy with judgments. But if mother and daughter be combined) HVI and HH, (then) is produced forth VV (or Microprosopus) as well as DV (or the androgyn, who also is a condition of judgments), for occultly Adam is denoted, or the male and female, who are that DV concerning whom it is written (in the place cited above) 'corrupt children.'

(When it is said) BRAShITh, BRA, *Berashith bera*, 'In the beginning created,' (the supernal paths are understood.) BRAShITh, *Berashith*, is the speech (one of the ten rules of Genesis), but BRA, *Bera*, is the speech halved.

(But there are here understood) Father and Son, the hidden and the manifest. (And also)

The superior Eden is hidden and concealed. (That is, no mention is made of the crown.) The inferior Eden comes forth so that it may be transferred (towards the inferiors) and manifested (through the voice of its original, which denotes wisdom.)

'No mention made of the crown'—i.e., Kether, the first Sephira, Macroprosopus.

For the name (Tetragrammaton) IHVH, *Yod, He, Vau, He,* includes the name IH, *Yah,* (which is of the father, and the name) ALHIM, *Elohim* (which here follows in the text, and pertains unto the mother).

ATh, *Ath* (the fourth word of this text, which in another manner signifies the name) ADNI, *Adonaï,* 'Lord' (namely, the path of the kingdom; also the name) AHIH, *Eheieh* (that is, the path of the crown, and thus symbolizes in itself the two extreme paths; here denotes) the right and the left (that is, benignity and severity), which are united in one (equilibrium).

Ath, ATh, means 'the,' 'the very substance of.' Qabalistically it signifies 'the beginning and the end,' and is like the term 'Alpha and Omega' used in the Apocalypse. For as Alpha and Omega are respectively the first and last letters of the Greek alphabet, so are Aleph and Tau of the Hebrew. The 'two extreme paths' are the crown, Kether, and the kingdom, Malkuth, the first and tenth Sephiroth, the highest and the lowest, Macroprosopus, and the queen. If the reader turns to the diagram showing the Sephiroth p.10, he will see that Malkuth is, as it were, the antithesis of Kether; and hence it is said that 'Malkuth is Kether after another manner.' And this recalls the precept of Hermes in the Smaragdine Tablet: 'That which is below is like that which is above, and that which is above is like that which is below.'

HShMIM, *Ha-Shamaim*, 'the heavens' (the fifth word of this text, and) VATh, *Vaath*, 'and the substance of' (the sixth word; they are referred to the paths of beauty and victory) like as it is written, 1 Chron. 29, 2 'And the beauty and the victory.' These paths are joined together in One.

The beauty and the victory' are Tiphereth and Netzach, the sixth and seventh Sephiroth.

HARTz, *Haaretz*, 'the earth' (the seventh word of this beginning denotes the queen joined together with the glory and the foundation), like as it is written, Ps. 8, 2: 'How magnificent (this is the path of glory) is your name in all the world' (whereby is symbolized the foundation); the earth which is the kingdom. Also) Isa. 6, 3: 'The whole earth is full of His glory' (where these three paths again concur).

'Let there be a firmament in the midst of the waters,' 'to make a distinction between the Holy Place and between the Holy of Holies.' (That is, between Microprosopus and Macroprosopus.)

The Most Ancient One is expanded into Microprosopus (or the Crown into the Beauty), and adheres to it, so that it may receive increase. If it be not perfectly expanded (so that Microprosopus as it were exists by himself, but instead is retained in his mother's womb) the mouth speaking great things moves in that place (that Microprosopus, so that he may be fully born), and he is crowned with the lesser crowns under the five divisions of the waters. (That is, Microprosopus receives the influx of the five benignities, which are called 'crowns,' because they descend from the crown, or Macroprosopus; but 'lesser crowns,' because they take their rise from benignity in the *Microprosopic path*; and they are called the five divisions of the waters, because the water belongs unto the benignity, and in this verse, Gen. 1, 6, 7, the word MIM,

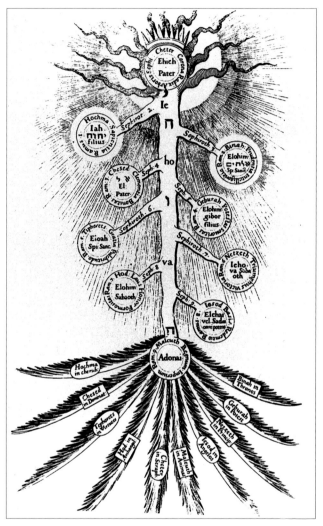

An interpretation of the Tree of the Sephiroth used by Robert Fludd in 1617 in his *Utriusque Cosmi Maioris*. The Tree is rooted in Heaven, so it is here upside down with the earth and its emanatiuons the 'flower' of the tree.

Meim, waters, fills the fifth place).

Like as it is written, Num. 19, 17: 'And shall pour upon him living waters in a vessel.' (But the life looks towards the mother; and it) is (understood to be that path which is called) ALHIM CHIIM, *Elohim Chiim*, 'the Elohim of life;' and the king of the universe (that is, the understanding. Where belong also the following sayings:—) Ps. 116, 5, 9: 'I will walk before the Lord in the lands of life.' Also 1 Sam. 29: 'And the soul of my Lord shall be bound in the quiver of life.' Also Gen. 2, 9: 'And the tree of life in the midst of the garden.' (All these, I say, refer to the understanding, from which the six members receive the influx. And to it also pertain the following names, namely, the name) IH, *Yah* (whenever it is written in full with A in this manner:) IVD HA, *Yod Ha* (and contains the number of the numeral powers of the letters of the Tetragrammaton, namely, 26; which is also referred to that form of the name belonging to the intelligence), AHII, *Eheii* (where in the place of the final *He*, *Yod* is put, as in a former instance. (See Chap. 1, p.15)

> In the Hebrew, CHIIM, *Chiim*, 'iving'; in our version of the Old Testament it is translated 'running water.' Chiim is plural.

Between the waters and the waters. (Since there are the superior) perfect waters, and (those which are in Microprosopus) imperfect waters (or those mingled with severities; because in another manner it is said) perfect compassion, imperfect compassion. (Now follows a mystical explanation of Gen. 6, 3.)

And the Tetragrammaton has said: 'My spirit shall not strive with man for ever, seeing that he also is in the flesh.' (In this passage, when it is said:) 'And the Tetragrammaton has said,' (it is to be noted that) after that there was formed (the supernal structure), in the last place concerning Microprosopus (this name is understood). For when it is said, 'He calls this also by the name,' the Ancient One speaks occultly in a hidden manner.

The Ancient One is symbolized by the pronoun He in the sentence, 'He calls this also by the name.'

'My spirit shall not strive with man.' (Here is understood, not the spirit of Microprosopus, but) that which is from the supernals, because from that spirit which rushes forth from the two nostrils of the nose of Macroprosopus the influx is sent down to the inferiors.

And because it is written (in the same place) 'And his days shall be a hundred and twenty years,' I, *Yod*, is either perfect (whenever its singular parts exist in the form of decads) or imperfect (when they are in monads or units). When therefore *Yod* is placed by itself) alone (it is understood to be perfect, because in itself it contains) a hundred. (But if) two letters (are put, then are understood the ten units) twice reckoned; (hence are produced) the hundred and twenty years.

The 'singular parts' of Yod are the numbers from one to ten, for the number of Yod is ten. But when Yod is taken as its square I x I = l0 x 10 = 100. But 11 = 1 x 1 + 1 +1 (or the two letters both multiplied and added together) = 10 x 10 +10 + 10 = 120. But when Yod = 100, its digits are tens and not units—namely, the numbers 10, 20, 30, &c., instead of 1, 2, 3. &c.

Yod is alone whenever he is manifested in Microprosopus (that is when the lights of Macroprosopus descend into Him, then indeed the paths of the decads are increased, and this decad) is increased into ten thousands (by the paths joined with the four letters of the Tetragrammaton) of years. (But) hence (if it be conceived only according to the power of Macroprosopus, it has that position) which is written, Ps. 139, 5; 'And you shall place upon me your hand:' KPKH, *Khephakha*. (Where this word KPKH, if it be written according to the usual custom KPK, *Khephakh* yields the number 120. But now by adding the paragogic H of the female, there is given the number 125, on account of the five severities.)

'This decad is increased into ten thousand by the paths joined with the four letters of the Tetragrammaton'—i.e., the paths are the Sephiroth = the numbers from one to ten; and they are said to be joined with the four letters by multiplying the decad to the fourth power, or 10^4. Hence for I, the first letter, we have 10 x 1 = 10; for H, the second letter, we have 10 x 10 = 100; for V, the third letter, 10 x 10 x 10 = 1,000; and for H, the fourth letter, 10 x 10 x 10 x 10 =10,000.

In the Shemitic languages, a paragogic letter is one which is added to a word to give it additional emphasis.

'There were giants in the earth,' Gen. 6, 4. (If this word HIV, *Hayu* is considered, which also is a form of the often varied name, it takes its rise from the kingdom.) This is that which is written, Gen. 2, 10: 'And thence is it divided, and is in four heads.' (Where is understood the end of that emanation which the separated universe follows. Nevertheless) from the place where the body is divided, they are called those trees (or, as the Mantuan Codex corrects the passage: Where the garden is divided, and the seven inferior emanations are understood; where then it divides the universe into the inferior worlds and provides a habitation for the shells or spirits of matter). Hence it is written: 'And from hence is it divided.'

'The shells' = elemental spirits. The Qabalah always calls the evil elemental spirits of matter 'shells.'

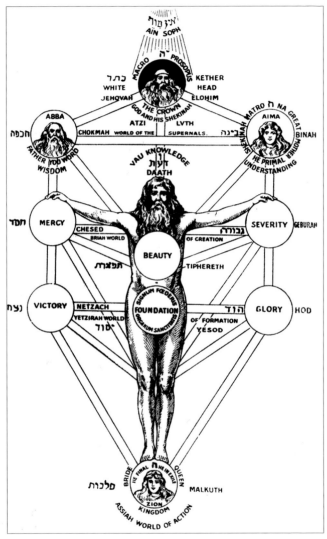

Another interpretation of the Tree of the Sephiroth from A E Waite's
The Holy Kabbalah published c.1860.

They were in the earth in those days, but not in the following time, until Joshua came. (That is, they are applicable to the path of the bride, which also is called the land of Canaan, wherein Joshua found the giants. For the word NPILIM, *Nephilim*, occurs not fully, except when it is used in the incident of the spies, Num. 13, 33.)

And the sons of the Elohim are guarded (nor is mention made of a similar case) until Solomon came and joined himself with the daughters of men; like as it is written, Eccles. 2, 8: VThONVGVTh, *Ve-Thonogoth* 'And the *delights* of the sons of men,' &c. Where (in the feminine gender) he calls the word ThONVGVTh, *Thonogoth*, and not (as elsewhere in the masculine gender) ThONVGIM, *Thonogim*, 'sons of Adam;' so that it is 'intimated in an occult manner that the latter (the sons of the Elohim) are of those other spirits who are not contained under the supernal wisdom; concerning which it is written, 1 Kings 5, 12: 'And the Lord gave wisdom to Solomon,'

Also it is written, *ibid.* 4, 31: 'And He was wise above every man.' Because these are not classed with man.

(But when it is said) 'And the Tetragrammaton gave him wisdom,' then is understood the supernal *He.* (Because he gave to him the influx of the wisdom of the queen.) 'And be was wise before every man,' because from her he received the wisdom here below (through the path to the kingdom).

Those (spirits) are powerful who exist from eternity. That is, from (eternity or) the supernal world (the understanding, namely, whence are excited severity and rigour). The men of the name (that is) who exercised themselves in the name.

In what name? In the Holy Name, wherein they exercised themselves (for the performing of various wonders), and not the holy inferiors. Yet (these) did not exercise themselves save in the name (and not in holiness).

It is said openly 'the men of the name,' and not 'the men of the Tetragrammaton.' Not (therefore used they the name) with respect to the mystery of the Arcanum, or in a diminutive form; nor yet with any diminution of the (name itself).

(And because) the men of the name (are) openly (spoken of, hence) are they shut out from the general conception of man.

It is written, Ps. 49, 12: 'Man being in honour, abides not.' (When it is said) 'man being in honour' (the same is as if also it were said, a man such as was Solomon) shall not remain long in the honour of the King without the spirit. (That is, in the influx from the King, Microprosopus, to whom, or to the beautiful path, the spirit belongs.)

Thirteen kings (that is, the twelve metatheses of the Tetragrammaton with its radix, which are the measures of mercies) wage war with seven (with the Edomite kings; because, while the lights of the former flowed down, these could not maintain themselves, and, besides, they are the classes of the most rigorous judgments which are opposed to the mercies. For) seven kings are seen in the land (Edom), and now after that their vessels are broken, they are called shells, who have fallen down among the inferiors. (These) nine vanquished in war (the measures of Microprosopus, concerning which see the *Idra Rabba*; through which David conquered his enemies), which ascend in the paths of those which pass downward, on account of His ruling power (that is, which make thirteen, as they are in Macroprosopus and his beard, which is called his influence, and freely flows down), and there is none who can withhold their hand. (For whilst the supernal measures permit the increase in the inferiors, all judgments are subdued.)

Concerning the 'twelve banners of the sacred Name,' the metatheses of the Tetragrammaton; also concerning the Edomite kings. I have before remarked that the demons are called Qlipboth, or 'shells,' by the Qabalists. The thirteen in Microprosopus is composed of nine manifest and four hidden.

'Five kings (that is, the five letters MNTzPK, *Me*, *Nun*, *Tzaddi*, *Pe*, *Kaph*, which are the roots of the judgments), betake themselves into swift flight before four (the four letters of the Tetragrammaton which bear with them the influx of benignity. They cannot remain (since the judgments and rigours cease and flee).

The letters of the Hebrew alphabet are divided into three classes, the three mothers as they are called, AMSh; the seven duplex letters, BGDKPRTh, so called because they are sometimes tenues and sometimes aspirates, according to whether they are written with or without the Daghesh point; and the twelve simple letters, HVZChTILNSOTzQ. They are also divided into the three categories of *Chesed*, *Din*, and *Ravhmim*, or mercy, judgment, and mildness. Now these five letters MNTzPK denote the severest judgments, and their number = 280 = PR = the name of the angel *Sandalphon*, SNDLPVN, the angel IOR, or of the wood of the world of Asiah, since the greatest part of it are sterile trees.

Four kings slay four (that is, the four letters of the Tetragrammaton are bound together with the four letters ADNI, *Adonaï*, which) depend from them like grapes in a cluster (in the concatenation of these two names, thus, IAHDVNHI).

Among them are set apart (that is, among these paths of the Divine names a selection of holiness is made from these broken vessels) seven channels (that is, seven broken vessels, which now are like the shells, and contain in themselves a great part of the lights and souls); they testify testimony (that is, the souls thus selected, thence having been

'In the beginning was the Word'. An eighteenth-century engraving.

born into the universe, testify that they are freed from impurity) and they do not remain in their place (and are no longer detained under the shells).

The tree which is mitigated (that is, the path of the kingdom or Schechinah, which is the tree of the knowledge of good and evil, which in itself exists from the judgments, but is mitigated by the bridegroom through the influx of mercies) resides within (within the shells; because the kingdom has its dominion over all things, and its feet descend into death). In its branches (in the inferior worlds) the birds lodge and build their nests (the souls and the angels have their place). Beneath it those animals which have power seek the shade (that is, the shells, 'for in it every beast of the forest does walk forth,' Ps. 104, 20).

This is the tree which has two paths (for thus is this passage restored in the corrected Codex) for the same end (namely, good and evil, because it is the tree of the knowl-edge of good and evil). And it has around it seven columns (that is, the seven palaces), and the four splendours (that is, the four animals) whirl around it (in four wheels) on their four sides (after the fourfold description of the char-iot of Yechesqiel (Ezekiel).

> The seven palaces answer to the 3rd, 4th, 5th, 6th, 7th, 8th, and 9th Sephiroth, operating through the respective orders of the angels into the spheres of the seven planets, Saturn, Jupiter, Mars, Sol, Venus, Mercury, and Luna. The four animals, or Chaioth Ha, Qadesch, are the vivified powers of the four letters of the Tetragrammaton operating under the presidency of the first Sephira as the mainspring of primum mobile of creation. The four wheels are their correlatives under the second Sephira, on their four sides—namely, the four elements of the air, fire, water, and earth, which are the abodes of the spirits of the elements, the sylphs, salamanders, undines, and gnomes, under the presidency of the tenth Sephira.

The serpent (which was made from the rod of Moses—that is, the shell—NVOH, *Nogah*, or splendour) which rushes forth with three hundred and seventy leaps (the thir-ty-two names together with the five letters of ALHIM, *Elohim*, which make 37, multiplied by the decad 370, and the judgments of the bride are denoted, to which that shell directs his springs, because he is of middle nature betwixt the holy and the profane). 'He leaps upon the mountains, and rushes swiftly over the hills,' like as it is written (Cant. 2, 8. That is, he leaps high above the rest of the shells). He holds his tail in his mouth between his teeth (that is, his extremity, by which he is linked to the shells, turns towards his other extremity wherewith he looks towards holiness). He is pierced through on either side (so that he may seek to receive the superior and inferior nature). When the chief arises (who is Matatron) he is changed into three spirits (that, is, he assumes the nature of three inferior shells).

'Nogah' is also the qabalistical title of the sphere of the planet Venus. MTTRVN, *Metatron*, or Methraton, is the particular intelligence of the first Sephira, and is called the 'Prince of Faces;' he is said also to have been the 'ruler of Moses.' Methraton has the same numeration as ShDI, *Shaddai*, the Almighty.

(But concerning Metatron) it is written, Gen. 5, 22: 'And Enoch walked with the Elohim' (because out of Enoch, Metatron is formed). And it is written, Prov. 22, 6: 'Enoch has been made into a boy, according to his path.' (That is, 'has been changed into') the boy (namely, Metatron, who is spoken of under his name NOR, *Nour*, which means a 'boy').

'Enoch has been made into a boy,' &c. This peculiar rendering of the passage, 'Train up a child in the way,' &c., arises from reading in the Hebrew text ChNVK, *Chanokh*, Enoch, instead of ChNK, *Chanekh*, 'train up,' or 'instruct.'

With the Elohim, and not with the Tetragrammaton (because he himself is referred to the path of the queen, to whom is attributed this name of Rigour). 'And he existed not' (longer) under this name (Enoch), because the Elohim took him in order that he might be called by this name. (For this name is communicable to the angels, and in the first instance to this chief among them, namely, Metatron.)

There are three houses of judgment given, which are four, that is, the three letters IHV, referred into the understanding, which yield the four letters of the Tetragrammaton, pointed with the vowel points of the name Elohim. For there are four superior houses of judgment (the four said Tetragrammatic letters) and four inferior (which are the four letters ADNI, *Adonaï*, belonging to the kingdom). For it is written, Lev. 19, 35: 'You shall not do iniquity in judgment, in dimension, in weight, and in measure.' (Where these four are mystically intimated.)

(There is one) rigorous judgment (of severity), another that is not rigorous (that is, of the kingdom). There is one judgment by balance (wherein are the two scales of merit and error), another judgment which is not made by balance; (and this is) the gentle judgment (whereby the Israelites are judged. But also there is given) the judgment which is neither of the one nature nor of the other. (Namely, the beautiful path.)

Of course the 'beautiful path' is Tiphereth, the sixth Sephira.

(Further on it is written), Gen. 6, 1. 'And it came to pass when man began to multiply upon the face of the earth.' (Where by these words) ADM, *Adam*, began to multiply (there is understood Daath, or the knowledge, the soul of the beautiful path, to which Moses is referred; which sends down many lights into the bride, the earth, when the spouse ascends thither). This is that which is written *(ibid.* 3): BShGM, *Beshegam*, 'in that also, he is flesh' (which word *Beshegam*, 'in that also,' by equality of numeration equals MShH, *Moses*) Adam (namely) the supernal (Daath, or knowledge). And it is written: 'Upon the face of the earth' (which face of the earth is this, that the highest representation of the queen is the understanding, the mother, to whose gates Moses ascended).

(Concerning this face, it is written) Exod. 34, 29: 'And Moses knew not that the skin of his face shone' where by the face the mother is understood; by the skin, the queen.) This is that which is said, Gen. 3, 21: 'Tunics of skin' (because by itself the kingdom is wanting in light).

To shine (but when it is said 'the face of Moses,' the

mother is understood), according to that passage, 1 Sam. 16, 13: 'And Samuel took the horn of oil' (where by the oil, the wisdom, by the horn, or the splendour of the oil, the understanding is denoted). For there is no anointing except by the horn (that is, every descent of unction is through the mother). Hence it is said, Ps. 89, 18: 'And in your favour our horn shall be exalted.' (Also) Ps. 132, 17: 'There shall the horn of David flourish' (that is, the queen shall receive the influx from the mother). This is the tenth of the kings (that is, the path of the kingdom), and originates from jubilee, who is the mother.

For it is written, Josh. 6, 5: 'And it shall be when the horn of jubilee is sounded.' This is the splendour of the jubilee, and the tenth (path) is crowned by the mother.

(This is) the horn which receives the horn and the spirit, that it may restore the spirit of *Yod He* to *Yod He*. (That is, when the spirit is to be given to Microprosopus, his mother contributed as much, which is QRN, *Qaran*, 'the horn,' the brilliancy, as the increase which he receives from the father.) And this is the horn of jubilee. And IVBL, *Yobel*, 'jubilee,' is H, *He* (the first *He* of the Tetragrammaton); and *He* is the spirit rushing forth over all (because the mother is the world to come, when in the resurrection all things will receive the spirit); and all things shall return to their place (like as in the jubilee, so in the world to come).

For it is written, AHH, IHVH, ALHIM, *Ahah Tetragrammaton Elohim!* 'Ah Tetragrammaton Elohim!' When the H, *He*, appears (first), and H, *He* (in the second place); then is Tetragrammaton called Elohim (like as a judge; because in the world to come there will be work for much strength. This is) the full name. And it is written, Isa. 2, 11: 'And Tetragrammaton alone shall be exalted in that day.' When the one *He* is turned towards the other

He, and *Yod* is taken away, then comes vengeance into the universe; and except for that Adam who is called Tetragrammaton, the universe would not exist; but all things would be destroyed. Hence it is written: 'And the Tetragrammaton alone,' &c.

Hereunto is the hidden and involved Mystery of the King, that is *The Book of Concealed Mystery*. Blessed is he who enters into and departs therefrom, and knows its paths and ways.

Family at Passover meal or Seder from a fourteenth-century Hebrew manuscript.

Glossary

ADAM: First created man by God. In their totality and unity the ten Sephira represent the architypal man, ADM QDMVN, *Adam Qadmon*, the Protogonos. *See* SEPHIROTH.

ADONAI (ADNI): Also known as the Divine Name or the Lord.

AIN SOPH: The hidden God and origin of all things. The cause of causes.

AMA: *Ama* is part of the third Sephira and makes up the supernal Trinity: *Ama:* Mother, *Aima:* the great productive Mother, and *Ab*, the Father.

ANCIENT ONE: Also known as *Authiqua*-incomprehensible and unseen. The first idea of equilibrium (the first Sephira or Crown Kether).

BINAH: The third Sephira or triad. Known as the Understanding it is co-equal with Chokmah.

CHESED: The union of the second and third Sephira. CHSD, *Chesed*, meaning Mercy and Love. Also called GDVLH, *Gedulah*.

CHOKMAH: The second Sephira CкKMH, *Chokmah* meaning Wisdom. *See* KETHER.

DALETH: The third letter D of the word IVD, *Yod.*

EDOMITE KINGS: When the earth was formless and void, these prior worlds are symbolised by the kings who reigned in Edom before there was a king of Israel.

ELOHIM: ALHIM, *Elohim.* Feminine form of God in whose image man and woman are created. According to the Kabbalah, woman is equal with man, and certainly not inferior to him. *See* HOA.

EQUILIBRIUM: The point within the circle of ancient symbolism, equilibrium is that harmony which results from the analogy of contraries. It is the dead centre where, the opposition of opposing forces being equal in strength, rest succeeds motion.

GEBURAH: The fifth Sephira meaning Strength and Fortitude.

GREATER HOLY ASSEMBLY: Also known as *Idra Rabba Qadisha* is another part of *The Zohar.*

HOA: HVA, *Hoa,* The mother of understanding. Also called ALHIM, *Elohim.*

HOD: The eighth Sephira meaning Splendour.

IDRA RABBA QADISHA: *See* GREATER HOLY ASSEMBLY.

IDRA ZUBA QADISHA: *See* LESSER HOLY ASSEMBLY.

IHVH: The four Hebrew letters which make up the Hebrew word for God. *See* TETRAGRAMMATON.

KABBALAH: *See* QABALAH.

KETHER: The first Sephira and Crown of the Sephiroth.

LESSER HOLY ASSEMBLY: also known as the *Idra Zuta Qadisha*, another part of *The Zohar.*

MACROPROSOPUS: Also known as the ARIK ANPIN, *Arik Anpin*, the Vast Countenance representing the Father of all things. He is partly concealed (in the sense of His connection with the negative existence) and partly seen as a positive Sephira. The symbolism of the Vast Countenance is that only one side of his countenance is seen. *See* NEGATIVE EXISTENCE.

MALKUTH: The tenth Sephira, MLKVTH, *Malkuth* meaning the Kingdom. The inferior Mother, Bride, Queen and Bride of Microposopus.

MANTUAN CODEX: An ancient document used to annotate the three most important parts of *The Zohar*, by Christian Knorr von Rosenroth (author of *Kabbala Denudata*, 1677).

MICROPOSCOPUS: The Lesser Countenance. Composed of the six of the Sephiroth that reflects the splendour of the Macroprosopus. Also referred to as the supernal Adam.

MOSES: In *c.* 1200 BCE God was revealed to Moses at the burning bush. He subsequently led the Hebrew tribes out of Egypt to the Promised Land. On the way the written Torah(Law) or Five Books of Moses and the oral Torah were revealed to him at Mount Sinai. *See* PENTATEUCH.

MOTHER: Female form of God. *See* ELOHIM.

NEGATIVE EXISTENCE: Cannot be defined. If it is it ceases to be negative existence. The Kabbalists believe that the AIN SOPH cannot be defined. The AIN, *Ain*, the negatively existent one is beyond comprehension. *See* POSITIVE EXISTENCE.

PENTATEUCH: The first five books of the Old Testament: Genesis, Exodus, Leviticus, Numbers and Deuteronomy. Also known as the Five Books of Moses.

POSITIVE EXISTENCE: Antithesis of negative existence. Capable of definition, having a beginning and end. *See* NEGATIVE EXISTENCE.

QABALAH: An alternative spelling is Kabbalah. The root meaning is 'received'. In Judaism the Kabbalah is the received (ie revealed and handed down as a mystical secret) inspired tradition of the mystical understanding of God and the Universe.

SEPHIROTH: Kabbalistic term for the 'regions' or 'spheres': the spirit, air, water, fire, the four cardinal points of the compass, height and depth. These ten Sephira are all emanations from God: the crown, the wisdom, the intelligence, the love, the power, the compassion, the steadfastness, the majesty, the foundation and the kingdom. All these are linked together as a vital organism, like a tree whose root is the Infinite, with the kingdom as the trunk, the foundation as the point from which the branches begin to spread, the compassion at the centre and the Crown (Kether) at the top.

TETRAGRAMMATON: Literally the fourfold lettering. In the Kabbalah the Hebrew name for God IHVH without the vowel points.

TIPHERETH: The sixth Sephira, THPARTH, *Tiphereth.* Meaning Compassion or Mildness.

VAU: The letter V. The shape of the Hebrew letter, *Aleph,* A (*See* Table on page 12) is said to symbolise a *Vau,* V, between a *Yod,* I and a *Daleth,* D. Therefore this letter represents the word IVD, *Yod. See* DALETH and YOD.

YESOD: The 'path of foundation', the ninth Sephira and sixth member of the Microprosopus.

YOD: The letter I which makes up the word IVD with a V, *Vau* and D, *Daleth.*

ZOHAR: Strictly *Sefer Ha-Zohar, The Book of Splendour,* but usually called *The Zohar.* Written in Castille towards the end of the thirteenth century it is said to be the work of Moses of Leon. The leading document of Jewish Kabbalism which consists of eighteen parts of which *The Book of Concealed Mystery* is one.